THE
RENEWED
MIND

REBUILDING TRUST IN MARRIAGE BY OVERCOMING PORN ADDICTION FOR LIFE

DR CHUCK CARRINGTON

This is a work of nonfiction. Some parts have been fictionalized to varying degrees, for various purposes.

2nd Edition

2nd Edition

ISBN 979-8-9892386-3-7

First printing edition 2023

Printed by Connect Books in the United States of America
Connectbooks.pub
PO BOX 903 Wakefield VA. USA 23888

Every effort has been made to trace or contact all copyright holders. The publishers will be pleased to make good any omissions or rectify any mistakes brought to their attention at the earliest opportunity.

All Pictures & Images Licensed by Pixabay
unless otherwise credited.

Table of Contents

A Special Thanks

Where to begin? There are so many people that caused this project to evolve into a successful program over the many years I have been in practice, people who will never be publicly known. Countless clients have formed and reformed my view of the struggle against porn, a permanent victory over the bondage of cybersexual addictions, and the recovery of the marriage trust and relationship. For the sake of confidentiality and dignity, none of them will be named. But their participation and contribution to others in our groups and in later applications of the work is invaluable. To you unsung authors goes the credit.

In the more practical sense, a team ultimately authored this book. Being excessively dyslexic myself, if it were not for the scrutiny of others, this book would be a shambles and unreadable. A special shout out to incredibly special friends for their help is warranted. I am grateful to Ryan Walden, Mike & Cindy Pray, Drew Maloney, David Marshall, and Hans Solum as the core team that made the entire program a success over the past few years with support, edits, insights, and wisdom. From you all I have learned a lot and tried to put your voices into this project.

I am also grateful to my mentor and friend, the *great professor* Dr Merrill Reese who taught me what it means to be present with people so that they can find healing. To Dr Nina Brown without whose help, I would have never understood narcissistic wounding, the many hidden dynamics of group processes and the best way to "shut up and listen" to the voice of the group. And to all the counselors, professors, colleagues, and mentors that I had the privilege to model my own practice after over the decades, thank you for being patient and kind.

Forward

By Mike Pray, Certified Coach

Dr. Chuck saved my life, saved my marriage, and saved my family. This may sound dramatic, but trust me, it is not. I have fought my addiction to pornography since my initial exposure to it 43 years ago. I am a good man that struggled with porn. I can say that honestly now because only in the last four years have I truly accepted and believed the absolute fact that I am indeed a good man. A good man that is worthy of God's forgiveness and love. I had tried the "just stop it" method, the "pray it away" method, and the "12 Step" method—all to no avail. After multiple discoveries that left my wife of 28 years wounded to her very soul, I began to seek counseling.

My church recommended an excellent family/marriage counselor that my wife and I attended weekly for a year. He was entirely unprepared for the type of wound my wife suffered from. Next, we sought out a specialist in sex addiction, a Certified Sexual Addiction Therapist (CSAT). His approach left me spinning in shame and hopelessness. I was placed in a box with all the other types of sexual addictions this world offers. When things were only getting worse instead of better, my wife found the name of the wound I gave her through a podcast, *Betrayal trauma*. The beast now had a name. I searched Psychology Today online and read every counselor narrative, and after 203 people, I found the first one that mentioned *betrayal trauma*: Dr. Chuck Carrington. And our journey to true healing began.

Dr. Chuck's work with my wife through all the pain and betrayal I brought her is a true gift. She would cry herself to sleep every night because of my actions. I made her look at herself differently, think about herself differently, and doubt every single thought she had about me and our marriage. He took that wounded, angry woman and brought her to a place of peace and forgiveness. Only when both parties are healed does the marriage survive.

Dr. Chuck uses a conjoint therapeutic method in his approach to helping the men and women struggling with this addiction. He works with the husband and wife separately in the first stage. This brings both parties to a place of healing and recovery before he works with them on the wounds one has inflicted on their marriage. His method exposes the damage that has been hidden and self-medicated through porn and then teaches you how to cope with and forgive the source of the pain. This achieves true freedom from the bondage of your sin.

Dr. Chuck offers several online men and women support groups, generally at no expense. These groups are based around a structured subject for that session, followed by intensive peer-to-peer support. This builds a community that strips the shame of the issue. The burden of the "I'm a monster, and I'm the only one doing this" thought process for the men brings the women together to work through the betrayal, and all the consequences of the addiction are stripped away. One group breaks down the behavior and thought patterns that lead you down this road and teaches you how to recognize those thoughts, feelings, and habits for the lies they are.

Dr. Chuck's passion is his work. This is his ministry. His compassion, empathy, insight, and courage to walk alongside people in the worst moments of their lives are the absolute definition of a godly and virtuous man. His self-sacrifice toward monetary gain, in a field often taken advantage of by others looking for a worldly payoff, is incredibly humbling.

I'll end as I began this; Dr. Chuck saved my life, marriage, and family. Mike Pray

Introduction

For years psychologists, social workers, and counselors have been split on the topic of whether or not porn addiction is real. But for any man who has struggled to break this addiction, and any woman married to a man who continuously betrays her due to his addiction, there is no question. Porn addiction is very real.

The addiction of the century that affects people across all demographics is *cyber-addiction*. Pornography, sexting, camming, emotional affairs, social media, gaming, and more all fall into this 21st century scourge. The addiction is real, the reasons are varied, and the damage to self and families, work and society, is just now being understood.

I began treating men and couples effected by porn addiction long before it became the latest thing in recovery. Over time, this work with men and their wives has allowed me to develop a treatment plan that works rapidly and has a long-term effect.

My program is founded on long-established values that support healthy relationships, applies the latest in neurobiological understandings of addiction, and intervention methods that provide psychoeducation and effective tools to break the cycle of cyber-based addictions.

Cyber-sexual addiction, particularly to porn, along with is counterpart, *Betrayal trauma* that impacts the spouses and relationships of the addict, is a significant portion of my counseling practice. Along the way to freedom from porn, the program addresses the communication blockages, *betrayal trauma* damage, and safety threats that couples experience from a man addicted to porn. I have found that there is little to gain in treating a cyber addiction if there is not an equal concern for the relationship and restoration of safety in the aftermath of *betrayal trauma.*

This book offers the addict and his spouse an opportunity to learn and apply the methods and tools I use daily with men from all over the world. Written in simple conversational language, you the reader can become an expert in your own recovery. This book along with the companion workbook contains the same materials, worksheets, and tools that I use for individuals and in my groups.

Am I Really a Sex Addict?

The short answer, probably not...

If you have read through the many different programs, books, and authors out there regarding porn addiction, you have likely been shocked and dismayed at the label "Sex Addict" being applied to you. Perhaps no worse label can be applied to someone that this. It connotes shame, weakness of character, shady sneaking around, elicit affairs, sick and twisted fantasies, the list goes on. The label will surely activate tremendous shame in you, and trigger your fight or flight response, pushing back against the label, much in the same way a chronic alcohol abuser recoils when labeled an alcoholic. But, where an alcoholic is addicted to alcohol, a porn addict is very often NOT addicted to sex at all.

So, are you a sex addict? Certain groups, theorists, and so-called experts called Certified Sex Addiction Therapists

(CSAT) would shout an absolute *yes* in your face. I say, Wait a minute. Let's consider this individual person, apart from a label, and see just what is happening here.

Surprisingly, as much as CSATs and popular long-running programs insist that porn addicts are in fact sex addicts, practical experience in counseling would disagree. Porn addiction is not about sex, at least not necessarily or in all cases. Yes, porn addicts can be sex addicts. Most sex addicts seem to also be porn addicts. But a porn addict is not *routinely* a sex addict. It happens, but it seems to be a rarity.

Porn addiction is about coping, stress management, habits from youth, and many other non-sexual origins. It typically forms during the teen years as the brain experiences daily changes due to exposure to many different stimuli. The fact that masturbation and sexual content is present doesn't make one a sex addict, any more than healthy marital sex does.

So why do some of the biggest programs insist on labeling porn addicts and users as sex addicts? Unfortunately, it is for a very simple reason. It's called *tradition*. Tradition is the adherence to a method or practice that has been used in the past, assumed to be the right thing to do, and is rather immune to change despite new evidence. For the same reason that scientists age fossils according to the *strata* of dirt the fossil is found in, despite compelling evidence that this isn't a reliable method, and likely dead wrong, CSATs and others label porn addicts as sex addicts. The original assumptions of the CSAT-based programs are no longer the most definitive voice in porn recovery, yet it is still used, promoted, even court ordered. The *assessments* that are used, the polygraphs that are applauded, and the treatment assumptions fostered are not evidence-based in supporting the labeling of most men as sex addicts.

My default is simple. Don't label without cause. It's unethical. I would estimate that 9 out of every 10 men I work with are NOT sex addicts, yet they are very addicted to behavioral processes that include porn use addictively. It's the label that really needs to be understood. For instance, we call a shopaholic a shopping addiction, not a product addiction, or stuff addiction. Shopaholics are addicted to the *process* of shopping. This may include stimuli such as finding deals and bargains, and is tied to the activity of shopping, not having stuff. Likewise, gambling addiction is not jackpotting addiction, it is the thrill of anticipation that the process brings along the way. A process addiction is an addiction to a process, not the outcome. Sex addiction is an addiction to sex; orgasming, intercourse, masturbation, etc. for the purpose of engaging in those activities for the sake of those activities. Porn addiction is named as it is because of the obvious connection that porn has to the dopamine drive, yet it is almost always about something entirely different: stress relief, excitement, escape, low self-image, power and control, curiosity, etc. The sexual component of porn addiction is not the reason men come back. It is for the escape from some other unpleasant condition that they engage in the process, just as a social media or phone addict can't stop posting and reading and surfing their apps. Are you as sex addict because you are a porn addict? Chances are high that you are not.

The Loss of Self

Doc, why can't I just quit? What is wrong with me?"

Every man who comes to my office seeking to break free from internet porn tells me that they have tried and failed, usually multiple times. Some say they quit on their own and made it six months or longer porn free, only to fall back into the habit without hope of ever being free. Others tell me they had assumed that once they were married with a normal sex life that they would no longer be compelled to visit porn sites. Despite a strong attraction for their lover and a satisfying sex life, they soon began to indulge once more. I have heard variations in both stories countless times. All of these men have one thing in common; they feel defeated, ashamed, and confused.

Porn addiction has become an epidemic in the 21st century, with estimates as high as 80% of men under 40 visiting a porn site weekly or more. Let us be honest, this is not the same porn your father or grandfather used, in the form of some magazine with naked or skimpily clad young women. This porn is insidious in its ability to overtake a man's mind and create a cycle, consuming many hours of video, pictures, texts, chats, or stories every week. Giving one of these men a playboy magazine would be met with indifference and boredom. Internet porn is so much more powerful. Younger men in high school or college report using porn daily, sometimes to obsessive levels. Often denied *existing* by many psychologists and counselors, internet porn use can become a true addiction.

So far, the American Psychiatric Association's book of disorders, the **Diagnostic and Statistical Manual,** 5th ed. (DSM-5), does not include porn addiction among its official diagnosis. However, the researchers who compiled the current version of the DSM-5 added Internet Gaming Disorder to their *Conditions for Further Study* as an emerging concern. Gaming disorder is being studied in multiple countries, with similar conclusions which demonstrate that gaming can become an addiction, disrupting the individual's ability to function effectively in life.

The same is seen in other behavioral addictions such as gambling addiction and shopping addiction. A look at the proposed cluster of symptoms for this proposed diagnosis of Internet Gaming Disorder is identical to what we see when treating persons who are porn addicted. Keep in mind that to be an addiction, the person does not have to demonstrate all the symptoms, just a cluster of them that support that addiction is present. Let us look at gaming disorder to explain what is happening with porn addiction. Here is a hint, they are the same disorder, with different content.

How Do You Know if It's an Addiction?

The DSM 5 for mental health diagnosis has identified symptoms of Internet Gaming Disorder:

- Preoccupation with gaming
- Withdrawal symptoms when gaming is taken away or not possible (sadness, anxiety, irritability)
- Tolerance, the need to spend more time gaming to satisfy the urge.
- Inability to reduce playing, unsuccessful attempts to quit gaming.
- Giving up other activities, loss of interest in previously enjoyed activities due to gaming.
- Continuing to game despite problems
- Deceiving family members or others about the amount of time spent on gaming.
- The use of gaming to relieve negative moods, such as guilt or hopelessness.
- Risk, having jeopardized or lost a job or relationship due to gaming.

Anyone familiar with porn addiction can immediately identify this list of symptoms as nearly identical to their own experiences. Most important, in determining if the use rises to the level of addiction, is whether the habit interferes with life functions such as work, personal relationships, time management, self-care, and the like. Along with those interferences come unwanted feelings of guilt, shame, or being out of control. Major symptoms strongly indicative of an addiction are:

- Needing an increased exposure to the addictive stimuli.
- Organizing life around addiction.
- Disregarding the consequences of using.

- Including close relationships or employment, taking risks so that the addiction can be experienced.
- Denying or deceiving in order to protect the addiction, and the presence of withdraw (anxiety, physical distress, or mood changes) when trying to discontinue.

Like all other identified addictions, these features are used to make the diagnosis of addiction.

The accepted symptoms for chemical and behavioral addictions share the following:

- Secretiveness, Lying, Stealing.
- Unexplained spending or charge card items.
- Changes in social groups, new and unusual friends, odd phone conversations or texting.
- Repeated unexplained outings or seeking alone time, often with a sense of urgency.
- Increased tolerance, needing to engage more with the addictive substance or behavior to get the desired effect.
- Withdrawal, when the person does not take the substance or engage in the activity, they experience unpleasant symptoms, which are often the opposite of the effects of addictive behavior.
- Difficulty cutting down or controlling addictive behavior.
- Activities are becoming more focused on addiction.
- Important social and occupational roles are jeopardized.
- Preoccupation with addiction: planning, engaging in, and recovering from addictive behavior.
- Extreme mood changes – happy, sad, excited, anxious, etc.
- Sleeping a lot more or less than usual, or at various times of the day or night.

The Bias Towards Sex Addiction

Despite sharing many of the same features as Internet Gaming Disorder, many psychiatrists, psychologists, and counselors continue to deny that there can be such thing as a *porn addiction*. This is in part to the cultural acceptance of porn use as a post-modern choice rather than a moral dilemma. The historic biases of specialists in *sex addiction* recovery also produces such denial. It is the prevalence of porn use that personally places a barrier of acceptance among the professionals who determine what is and is not a diagnosable malady. Whatever the reason, the denial of the reality of porn addiction only provides an excuse to those addicted to continue their porn abuse.

What do we know about internet porn addiction that can help us break the cycle? Porn addiction is unique in how it affects the user. Unlike chemical addiction, there is no true end goal or high that drives the addiction like when someone shoots up a drug. With substances, the actual introduction of the substance into the body brings on the high, which then dissipates over time as the user comes down from their high. All activities that support addiction are designed to get the person to that state of escape through the high.

Sex addiction is more like a drug addiction than *porn addiction* would be. For the sex addict, it is the act of sex that is sought and satisfies the urges by providing the actual high. The outcome for sex addiction is in the final act—sexual release. While porn addiction has its own sexual component, sexual release is not the final act that drives the addiction. In fact, the sexual release is most often delayed as long as possible in porn addiction, so that the *process* of using the porn is extended. This is the reason we can say with confidence that internet porn addiction is NOT sex addiction. It is an entirely different type of addiction known as a *process addiction*.

Process Addictions focus on the process involved, not the outcome. Commonly known process addictions would include gambling addiction and shopping addiction. When a gambling addict or shopaholic engages in their addiction, they are not necessarily seeking a jackpot, or the acquisition of novel items. They are excited by the process of getting there. The gambler experiences his high when *anticipating* a possible big win and is seldom deterred by a big loss. The process is all that matters. This stimulation of the reward center is why a gambling addict can continue the process of gambling despite the reality of a long losing streak that leads them to total ruin. The same goes for a shopaholic. They do not need added items. In fact, many have hordes of products with the tags still on at home that they never use. They are engaged in the process of shopping, a form of *hunting*, not in having.

The process that internet porn addicts crave is much the same as gamblers and shoppers. I call it *the hunt*—the process of seeking out and finding new and exciting videos or pictures, collecting or reviewing them, while continuously searching among the variables to find that perfect sample. Once found, they are satisfied that they have what they want, and have had enough stimulation. At this point they stop delaying their bodies urges and masturbate to orgasm.

It would seem the orgasm is the end goal, but that would be wrong. Many porn addicts never choose to achieve an orgasm, some cannot. Yet they continue the hunt regardless of the outcome. It is this hunt that drives them, and now you know why. With this repetition of the hunt ending in satiation, building dopamine continuously along the way, the addiction is developed.

This form of addiction occurs when the brain is given a continuous reward via a certain substance or process that it can rely on for a *Dopamine* reward. Process addictions use the dopamine reward system in the same way a substance abuser uses alcohol or drugs. All addictions, substance or process, abuses the dopamine reward center affect. But in process addiction, there is a process, not a chemical or a definitive outcome, that triggers dopamine and if this process is prolonged it is like a dopamine drip that can be maintained at an extended high.

When gambling addicts are studied using fMRI brain imaging the affects can be mapped. The known addict is shown visual stimuli that triggers his gambling process yearning. Blood surges to the brain lighting up those accustomed pathways which promise reward. The dopamine is stimulated in the brain. It is not the jackpot that does this. No jackpot is offered. It is the stimulation of anticipation that triggers dopamine. So long as there is *anticipation*, the high continues.

The dopamine reward center is our pleasure center. The purpose is to use pleasure to reinforce learning, as well as to reward effort towards achieving. It also tends to promote more impulsivity in seeking new options that satisfy the desire for pleasure. The dopamine inducing pathway connects with other parts of the brain over time to create neuropathways where reward is predictable and is reinforced. As the brain builds these pathways, the person learns to modify their behavior over time. The major integration of such pathways is referred to as the reward system. Various regions of the brain form integrated circuits.

The process looks like this. The amygdala produces positive or negative emotions which create our emotional memories. The hippocampus retrieves and processes memories. Then the prefrontal cortex determines how to assemble those memories and feelings into behavior. As a result, the rather complex reward system connects these major sub-systems together to regulate our pleasure, reward efforts, and to motivate future actions, all from memories, and then to motivate us to attend to the things that it has *identified* as useful to us or as necessary to survival.

Some behaviors are naturally reinforced because they assure our survival. A baby learns to eat due to the need-reward experience. Later, to cry out when his need is noticed to achieve this reward on demand. Likewise, we seek companionship, sex, and other survival needs. Our behavioral choices that take us to our goal swiftly and assuredly are the patterns we incorporate into our reward pathways.

This system is normally established by the time the brain reaches full maturity, sometime in the twenties. In adolescence, the system is still highly malleable, with the prefrontal cortex changing daily as new experiences occur and require processing. This makes adolescent children highly susceptible to the stimulation of the reward system. It is there to teach and reinforce learning. But certain stimuli that is beyond their capacity to comprehend or cope with, *Supernormal*

Stimuli, creates too much change, and can usurp the normal development, especially when drugs, sex, or other highly addictive stimuli is applied.

In my work, I have found that more than 95% of porn addicts report that their addiction is rooted in exposures around ages 10-12. Their brains became hijacked to the addiction long before they knew the danger existed. To them, it was simply a curiosity and exciting new discovery. But their brains adapted to the stimuli as life giving and affirming, setting up the need and craving for continued feeding.

When you understand the nature and purpose of the reward system, it is easier to understand the power of addiction. Addiction occurs when the reward system has been hijacked to seek this *one source* of pleasure ahead of all others, creating a life disruption. Keep this system in mind as you work through this book and program. It is this system that will fight you, and this system we are actually working to treat therapeutically, to alter and recover.

Our Three-Stage Model of Recovery

A process addiction is a neurobiochemical based reaction to learned behavior through positive reinforcement, often originating from normal compulsive actions such as sex, masturbation, social reinforcement, or other outcomes that are deemed desirable. The repetition of the behavior which results in the release or flooding of the brain with endorphins

---

3-Stage Addiction Process:

1. Brain flooded with unlimited or *supernormal* stimuli.
2. Dopamine reward system is hijacked.
3. Isolation from obstacles that threaten to interrupt the stimulus supply.

3-Stages of Porn Addiction:

1. Normal process of discovery of sexuality and self.
2. Process altered by exposure to supernormal or ubiquitous stimuli via porn.
3. Negative or incomplete brain development of perspectives on sexuality reinforced by repetitive porn use.

3-Stage Process of Breaking Free:

1. Cease flooding the brain with stimuli to reduce dopamine reinforcement.
2. Disconnect shame messages, false identity, and faulty adaptations for coping.
3. Reconnect to self and a proper view of relationship to God, Self, and Others

---

(pleasure chemicals) can lead to the development of an addictive cycle which, when unbroken, progressively worsens.

Often these cycles originate with binge events, where intoxication is maintained or rehearsed excessively. In the case of internet porn, about ninety five percent of my clients describe early adolescent access to pornography during the time they are becoming sexually aware, combining it with frequent and sustained masturbation. The rehearsal of the porn-masturbation connection ties the reward to the process. The teen subconsciously discovers it takes more stimulus or more time to achieve the peak excitement first experienced. As the practice of self-enticement evolves, typically with increased stimulation by delaying orgasm, the result is a flood of dopamine to the reward center of the brain. This creates a strong positive reinforcement of the behavior which is attempting to relive the initial flood of reward that occurred in the first exposure to porn with masturbation.

At the earliest stages of development of what will become the addiction cycle, there is an impulsivity which redirects the teen, using this new method of positive reinforcement, which quickly becomes irresistible. The result is addictive-related learning associations which set up a lifetime belief or mental fusion. When neurons in the brain are connected in response to a behavior which is rehearsed, neuroplastic changes occur as the continued release of dopamine leads to an increased dynorphin levels. Dynorphin changes stress responses, alters feelings of dysphoria, and is linked in many of the system's ability or inability to manage life challenges. It has a *tamping* down effect on the person's euphoric feelings. Dynorphin decreases the effect of dopamine on the reward system, which in turn decreases the reward experienced and increases tolerance to the stimuli. This is the reason addicts must continue to seek more stimulation to replicate the high they experienced at the beginning. The cycle requires an ever-increasing level of stimulation to bring about the reward and in doing so, reinforces the cycle.

Research has found that many 21st century internet activities are becoming addictive due to their capacity to deliver *unending stimulation*. The unlimited content of the internet promises never-ending new experiences at a simple click of a mouse. This capacity is the stuff addictive dreams are made of. An inexhaustible source of addictive stimuli available at anytime and anywhere. We see the result of internet addictive potential in practices like engaging in social media, checking text messages, or viewing likes on Facebook, tracking Twitter content, being obsessed by the number of followers or views received, and the ability to know the answer to any question in a moment. Researchers suggest that the internet provides supernormal stimuli to those whose brains have already succumbed to addiction-related changes. Tinbergen[1] (1989) proposed the concept of supernormal stimuli as "a phenomenon wherein artificial stimuli can be created that will override an evolutionarily developed genetic response."

Now perhaps the answer to why it is so hard to quit is beginning to reveal itself. It is not a matter of willpower. The brain has been altered, from early adolescence, to require continuous stimulation from never-ending porn to satisfy a craving that is deeply rooted in the dopamine reward system. Without that reward the user has no sense of peace. The mental fusions are strong because they are so well used.

This makes recovery very difficult from the traditional perspective used in certain programs, often preferred in church and community programs. The focus on the sinfulness of a behavior, while true and necessary, will not help the person whose entire life history from adolescence has been both mentally and chemically altered to *need* certain activities to cope. In many of my couples' sessions, I have to tread carefully on this topic because there are two realities at work.

One is choice. Chosen behavior that is sinful must be addressed as sin and viewed in light of the consequences of that sin. But there is an illness of sorts (altered brain functioning) that is also present that requires healing, not confrontation. When a spouse is hurt and mad about the choice issues, she is unlikely to empathize with the illness problem of an altered mind. When the addict is defensive because his source of coping is being threatened, he is unlikely to be able to address the complexities of sin and relational damages in the moment. There requires a balanced and complete approach to this dilemma.

Complicating the matter is the usurping of the addict's pair-bonding instinct, their stress management coping strategies, social conformity, deep feelings of shame and other factors which all work together to create a firewall of defense against breaking free. Like all addictions, internet porn addiction fights to stay in control, resisting all efforts to extinguish it. The brain under continued stimulation will suffer strong withdrawals when the stimulus ends. Addicts can experience anxiety, panic, fear, threat, and many other emotional responses.

Is it any wonder that this addiction is so hard to break? Unlike alcohol or drugs, there is no 21-day detox of the chemical stimuli. The chemicals are produced in the brain, are reinforced by memories and images deeply embedded, and upheld by instinct for sex, companionship, and affirmation. Porn detox takes many months, a year or more for many, to break down the mental fusions, those superhighways to pleasure that are so well known, and extinguish the addictive hold on the victim.

To break out of a belief system, you first must start by replacing certain core thoughts that uphold the faulty belief system supporting your porn addiction or cyber-sexual use. In their famous book, Ken Blanchard and Spencer Johnson[2] effectively identified a process of challenging and replacing faulty behavior that leads to wrong outcomes. They did so with a focus on setting the right goals, and intentionally working on those goals. Addiction recovery works in much the same way. The actual goals of addiction may be hidden long before you realize an addiction has taken hold. Many were there for a purpose that seems so far unrelated to your current struggle that you may be unaware of the driving force of your addiction. I have had men in session who have discovered goals of excitement, curiosity, stress relief, significance, control, relaxation, revenge, escape, and collecting.

These needs are driven by individual experiences while growing up. We call this the *phenomenology* of life. Every person is unique to a great degree in how he experiences and processes events. So, every life is a phenomenon. Life instructs you as you live it. To be optimally successful, a boy or young man must experience life and simultaneously have guidance from a well-integrated man to help him understand and define what he is experiencing. This is the purpose of a father.

Unfortunately, many boys do not have a father or do not have a father that takes on the role or has a father that never received guidance in his own youth. When this occurs, the boy learns to identify and organize his life phenomena by personal interpretation or by the dictates, fears, and traditions of other boys around him. This is where life views become relative to the world in the moment, rather than by well-constructed outcome-based perspectives. When raised by a single mom, or primarily by women, boys do not learn about masculinity and are stunted in growth. The only way out seems to be to emulate other's behavior. However, emulation without understanding can lead to disastrous results, and a very warped view or maleness.

Over time, life starts to condition men into believing a cluster of myths that become stereotypes. Some of those myths fit exactly into Blanchard and Johnson's identified process. First on the list is the conflation of worth and behavior. While behavior does say a lot about character and the internal thought-feeling process, it does not make or break a person's worth. All people are of immense worth, even though all people fail miserably at times. When external behavior begins to define your own worth, the result is shame.

Shame is a corruption of God's gift of guilt. Guilt says, *I did* a dreadful thing. It is there to help you not do it again. Shame says *I am* a dreadful thing. Shame robs you of your healthy love for yourself. So, first things first—stop assigning worthlessness to your own identity and target your disappointing behaviors for change. If you are like most men, you struggle with some of these internal messages. Most men struggle with them because we have all learned to accept grand myths about manhood and our place in the world over time.

Second, to deal with negative or sabotaging behaviors you must set a goal. All behavior follows a goal. When the goal is wrong, you will not have the behavioral outcome you want. And if those problematic behaviors continue, there will be consequences, often negative, sometimes rewarding, which will influence your future behaviors.

Over time, behavior begins to show as a pattern of habit and character. Character is nothing more than an outward expression of internal thoughts, feelings, and decisions to act. The trap is in the habits that you form in that process. As time wears on, you will become convinced that you are indeed your behavior. That myth has taken down many men.

The truth is, you are not your behavior, you are a man who is learning to manage his behavior. You are on a journey to tame the fallen nature that you were born into and replace your base character with one that is more civilized, righteous, and loving. The fastest way to get there is to closely examine your goals, your real goals, and then see how they are influencing behaviors. If your outcomes are not what you want, examine the goals you have abandoned. If your behavior is not what you want, revise your goals, or reactivate lost ones so that your behavior will match them, and change your life.

Choices Determines Outcomes

Wherever you are today, it was determined by The Cognitive Behavioral process:

The CBT formula: A + B = C

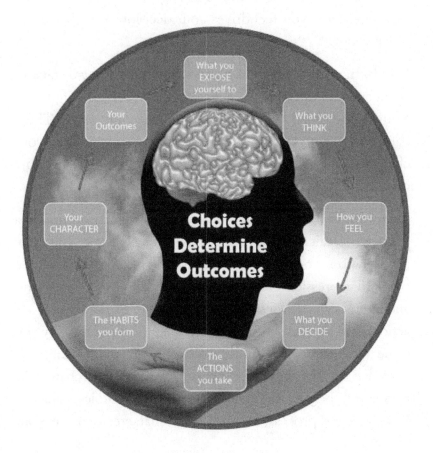

A = **Thoughts.** It begins with *exposure*. Environments, music, movies, friends, family culture, politics, religion, and more will determine how you *think*. We become immersed in our lives, and what we engage with has an impact. Your beliefs are influenced by your exposures. It is belief or points of view that direct how you think about a given situation.

B = Feelings: How you think determines how you *feel*. If you believe that something is unfair, you may then feel cheated. So, the first step is to alter your exposure. Choose to resist those things that are harmful and engage in positive healthy exposure. How you feel drives your decisions on what to do about events.

C = Behaviors: Those *decisions* tell you what *action* to take to change or manage your feelings and the events driving them. Your actions tend to be repeated and become *habits*. These habits that you create determine your *character*. And your character will produce *outcomes* which amplify exposure. The cycle continues to reinforce itself.

Many people believe that character is an inborn quality or a personality trait that does not change over a lifetime. This view is both wrong and misinformed. Character is no more than the outward expression of our inward process used to understand and interact with the world. It is highly visible to others in your actions and choices, but it is also visible to you in the way you came to those actions and choices. So, character, being the evidence of the inward process, can and will change as exposures, beliefs, thoughts, feelings, and choices change. Change your process, change your character, change your outcomes.

You are feeling what you're feeling because you're thinking what you're thinking.

Changing your cognitive behavioral cycle:

Your mind - not just your behavior - must change. God calls to resist behavior that does not honor Him. Instead of focusing only on outward behavior, learn to discipline your mind, altering behaviors. Allow God to transform you by the renewing of your mind (Romans 12:2). Change your situation or the outcomes you face, by breaking the cycle—simply reverse the process. Identify where things are going wrong, finding the dissonance, the disconnect between what you want, and what you do.

Cognitive dissonance is a psychological term to describe the anxious stress that occurs when thoughts, beliefs, or attitudes are inconsistent with behavioral decisions, outcomes, or life events. What you believe about some event tells you what to think. If you act out in a way that violates your core beliefs, you will feel guilt, shame, disappointment in self. Finding the disconnect is easier when you look at your process in reverse order. Starting with the part you feel is not what you want.

Reversing the process:

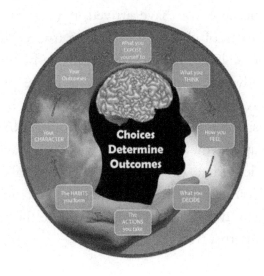

- If you do not like your outcomes, change your character,
- If you do not like your character, change your habits,

- If you do not like your habits, change your actions,
- If you do not like your actions, changes your decisions,
- If you do not like your decisions, change how you feel,
- If you do not like your feelings, change how you think,
- If you do not like how you think, change what you believe.
- If you don't like what you believe, change what you expose yourself to.
- If you do not like what you are exposed to, change your immediate choices and thereby take every thought captive (2 Corinthians 10:5) protecting your heart, "let your heart not be troubled," (John 14:1) but instead learn to prosper your soul, and in doing so, your life and your walk will prosper.

Taking back your Power means taking Ownership of your choices

When life gets tough, you may choose to believe that you are a victim of outside forces—that it is not your fault, and therefore, you can be angry at others. This belief is a faulty one because you have arrived at your circumstances through a series of choices. Other than true victimization, most of the time bad outcomes are avoidable by making good choices in advance. Choosing wisely is to be proactive, not reactive. When taking ownership of your bad choices, you will simultaneously regain your power. No longer do others act upon you against your will. You have the power to self-determine. Change your beliefs by challenging them, and soon you will find you like where you are, what you feel, and how you think. Your character will be the external proof of your internal truth.

If you are in counseling, ask your counselor to work with you on taking ownership by working through your cognitions and beliefs. You will quickly discover that what you believe really does determine what actions you are taking that lead you to make choices. If you do not like your mood, attitudes, habits, character, or outcomes, you can change them!

It is easier than you think. So often we find ourselves in situations where life is handing out stressful events that drive us toward being overwhelmed. We find ourselves becoming depressed, frustrated, even angry. It seems that all too often we get stuck in circumstances that make us unhappy, rob us of peace or joy, and make life difficult. Unfortunately, we tend to get to these places because we are making choices that take us there. The source of our personal misery exists in the basic choices we make, driven by a predictable cycle. So, if you genuinely want to change your situation, you must look to the true source of your unhappiness.

Change the Source, Change the Result.

1. You are where you are because of choices. Happily-ever-after is a myth that we all learn in childhood. There is no "and they lived happily ever after." Life is not that simple. Happiness cannot be a destination, because happiness is no more than a momentary outcome of other factors. A destination is a place where you can arrive and if you choose, remain. Happiness is not a place, it is a state of mind, of being, of attitude, but not a place. When you make the mistake of judging your life by the presence of happiness, more often than not, you will find something to be unhappy about at any given time. That something will tell you that you are not happy, and soon, you become

discouraged. Happiness is transient, elusive, and temporary.

2. Choices are yours to make. Nearly all your circumstances are a result of choice. Some of those choices are far in the past, some are subtle, and you may not even notice. But they were there at some point, and in some way caused the present to turn out the way it has. Most people are resistant to the idea that it was their own choice that has produced their misery.

3. Ownership. Unfortunately, resistance to ownership makes change extremely hard. In reality, refusing to accept ownership of choice and outcomes abdicates your power to others or to chance. This is called taking a victim stance—as if circumstances or other people are at fault for your personal outcomes. If that were true, then it would mean that you have no power over your life. That simply is not true. It is your life, and your job is to determine how it works out. Ownership brings back your power, even it if an admission that you are the cause of much of your own unhappiness. Ownership starts by first admitting to yourself that you made choices that brought you to a place that you do not like. Accounting for choices is not pleasant, but it is empowering.

4. Change is difficult, but doable. Change is the only constant in life. Everything changes over time. Yet, change is the one thing that all human beings seem to fear most. Change, even good change, requires some level of loss. The old ways are discarded, old familiar people, places, or things are replaced, or old habits are abandoned for new. Change can be frightening, hard, or full of ambiguity. Many simply choose to continue in the same old habits and instead cope by complaining about their circumstances. But change is in your power. You simply have to choose differently. It might not be easy, but it is doable.

5. Outcomes are predictable. Wherever you find yourself struggling in a given moment it is due to specific choices you have made, choices you may not even be aware of. Some choices are good, some bad, and some just set up happenstance. It is the major choices that you make that should concern you. Those choices will set up a process which will lead to certain outcomes. Much of the time, these outcomes are predictable.

6. Rumination is running a thought over in your mind repeatedly. When focused on negative or unpleasant thoughts or outcomes, your mood becomes altered. Rumination can make you *feel* powerless. Powerlessness tells you that you are stuck in or with something you do not like. Yet what you are *stuck* with is a result of some prior choices. If you *choose* yourself into becoming stuck, you can just as easily *choose* to become unstuck.

Accountability Is the Key to Change.

Extreme examples often help us see what is invisible in a more normal context. Let's use an extreme example to clarify how choices and accountability work. In the world of criminal offense, offending behavior that repeats are called recidivism. This word is used to describe when an offender commits new and repeated offenses, often indicative of a pattern. Most repeat offenders have an identifiable *offense cycle*. Statistically, they tend to repeat their offenses at a high rate, between 44% and 83%. Sexually based offenses are in that statistic too, but most people assume that it is higher and incurable because culture tells us that these offenders suffer from an immutable and uncurable character flaw. However, extensive long-term research from all angles and political sides have shown that those convicted of sexual offenses do not reoffend more, or even as much, as other crimes. Why? Because those convicted of sexual crimes are typically mandated into counseling which focuses on the cognitive behavioral process and high levels of accountability. While *untreated* sexual reoffending levels look much like any other offense, post-treatment reoffending is statistically and dramatically lower than any other crime.

Looking only at sexual offending, which is also a *process addiction* in most cases, we find that once treatment is completed, counseling is engaged in, psychoeducation has been provided, and accountability is present, less than 4% of sexual offenders ever reoffend. This is an amazing statistic for criminal recidivism. No other group has this low of risk to the public for re-offense. This is because it is *treated as an addiction* as well as *a process of cognitive behavioral choice*, not as a simple character flaw or immutable illness as it once was. If this can happen for sexual offenders in the criminal system, it can happen for any process addiction!

Fix, Don't Shame

Shame is also a major faction in the axis of evil that makes up the *Hated Enemy*. It develops from the messages we received while growing up. Let us look at some of those messages that you may have integrated into your own heart and mind.

Take a moment and consider some of the outcomes in your life that you do not welcome. Using the Cognitive Behavioral Cycle above as your guide, work the cycle backwards and determine where and why your outcomes were set into motion.

What did you learn about masculinity growing up?

Explicit messages are those that are out in the open, direct, and obvious. One of the earliest that most men recall is "big boys don't cry." Variations on this one theme would include "don't be such a baby." Or "stop being so sensitive." Or "toughen up."

1. Using the bullet list below, list out the explicit messages taught to you by your:
   - Parents
   - Grandparents
   - Siblings
   - Friends
   - Teachers
   - Mentors
   - Society
   - Others

Implicit messages are ones that are discerned, figured out, or reworded or punished without necessarily being made explicit. Think about how your father may have done the heavy lifting for your mom, opened doors, ignored her crying, insisted on dinner at a certain time, refused to do household chores, or pushed you out of the way when he was busy. All of these actions speak into the child's good or bad lessons. They become part of our implicit messaging, internal rules of masculinity.

2. Do the same for the Implicit messages taught by:
   - Parents
   - Siblings

- Friends
- Teachers
- Mentors
- Society

Guilt is a tool we use against others and against ourselves. The art of guilt is learned just like other messaging. If guilt is used on a child, that child might become highly shame based. When guilt stops saying, "what you just did was wrong" and instead becomes "you are a wrong person" shame takes root. Shame can become toxic to a child and will control that child when he becomes an adult.

Consider:

How you might use your natural guilt in a healthy way, while rejecting the toxicity of shame.

Willpower is Not the Answer!

Somethings are bigger and more powerful than you. It is impossible for most men to white knuckle their way into overcoming a cyber-based porn addiction. If you have chosen to become a part of one of our recovery groups, it is safe to assume that you already know this immutable truth. It is true that many, even most, can achieve temporary sobriety on their own. Some report going for as long as a year or more without relapsing back to porn. But then, for some reason or another, they do fall back into their old habits and begin the cycle of shame and defeat all over again. While the individual person may not recognize the reason, there is always a connection to the past and an identifiable cycle, driven by that old friend dopamine. To break the cycle, you must first know what it is, and how it overtakes you.

Willpower will not work because the drive to gain a dopamine surge through the addiction is *stronger* than the cognitive goal of sobriety. It is as simple as that. You will never overpower addiction with simple willpower. It takes pain, knowledge, and support to make this type of change. Most of all, it takes a bigger and more powerful end result that you desire more than anything else. This then is one of our group goals, to find the one thing bigger than cyber-sex that will draw you to it like a starving man is drawn to a McDonalds.

Shame Activates and Willpower Fails.

Shame is used in many contexts, but in the context of recovery and self-esteem, shame is toxic. Think of it as a corrosive word. It eats away at the substance of your soul, your self-identity, your image. Shame is one of the members of the *Axis of Evil* that makes up your *Hated Enemy*. Shame is quite different from guilt. Guilt is that feeling of conviction that comes when we realize we have done something wrong, bad, or which violates our values. Guilt is useful when it says, "I have done a dreadful thing. I must not do that anymore." The feeling of guilt, along with the cognition of conviction turns a reasonable person from wrongdoing. Shame, on the other hand, says something altogether different. It is not "I've done something bad." Shame says, "I am bad," and that is something we naturally recoil away from. When shame appears, fight of flight mode activates in half a heartbeat. Defending image, pushing the thought away, or fighting off the dread of shame is automatic, and for many men, well-rehearsed. For this reason, shame is included as part of the *Hated Enemy*.

Men are highly vulnerable to shame messages. This is actually encoded into men's biological response to the world, to relationships, and to joining, but it is heavily reinforced by how men and boys are taught to socialize. Shame is a natural go to whenever a man perceives he is failing in some capacity. But men can counter that tendency to go to shame by challenging many of the messages and assumptions that are inculcated in growing up. The expectations of conformity to male culture are demanded of all boys by other boys, by siblings, parents, and society. Because of this, boys demand it of themselves, and men fight to maintain the presentation of well-established maleness.

In the post-modern world of the day, some have tried to label maleness as *toxic masculinity*. But that is extending male conditioning into an illness or pathology, which it is not. Maleness is an identifiable quality that is valued in all cultures in some way. Maleness is both biologically driven and socially reinforced. While in some cultural sense some might take it too far, it is nonetheless an essential part of identity.

There are implicit messages that are also taught or learned along with the development of maleness in life. One of those is, if you show failure or weakness, you are less than, and are deserving of ridicule or shame. Some of this shaming is subtle. Parents continue to teach their boys to be tough, knowing that toughness will be demanded of them in the difficult adult world. Implicit in some common teaching such as "big boys don't cry" is the message, if you cry, you are not a big boy, i.e., you are not being manly. While this seems like a small issue, it is at the root of male pride, and male shame.

If you grew up among other males, you know what I am talking about. Show emotion openly past a certain age, often an incredibly young age, and the other boys, the girls, and many adults will react. Shaming is the application of a message of being inappropriate in self, not just behavior wrong. Big boys do not cry is not telling a boy to stop crying as a result of efforts to teach self-soothing and a healthy cognitive evaluation of his emotional state. It is telling them that they are *not being manly*, and therefore, they are *inadequate*, a *failure*, and *unacceptable* as a man.

If as a teen, and you were to cry openly, you would risk public scorn, shame, ridicule, shunning, even physical attack. Other boys, who are also taught to fear emotions, will target aggression on other's unacceptable expressions, in reaction to their own inner fear of shunning and potential shame if they were to ignore or allow such inappropriate displays of anti-maleness. Male pride is all about not being seen as weak and vulnerable, in defense against potential attack by the group. Male pride is different from false pride or pridefulness. It is fear of being found inadequate or failing the test of being male.

My goal here is not to critique social conditioning. Only to understand the role it plays in the war against cyber-sexual abuse. It is enough to know that this problem of reaction to suggestions of inadequacy is enough to trigger a strong shame response to as close to 100% of males as is statistically possible. It is not something you will be able to just shut off. It is a part of who you are, established long before you can remember. With this in mind, we will fight the acceptance of shame, not the underlying social conditioning that undergirds it.

Accountability is Necessary

Accountability is necessary. This simple statement about accountability becomes a major point of departure for many men who seek to defeat cyber-sexual addictions and abuse. The topic of porn has become acceptable in contemporary society, falling out of the mouths of everyone in a casual mention. However, when it comes to discussing an individual's use of porn, there remains a personally vigilant taboo. To joke about it or discuss it in theory is easy. To say, *"I have a problem with porn"* is a whole other issue. The difference is shame. Moreover, shame is the reason so many men refuse accountability in many of its forms, and why accountability is absolutely vital to defeating porn completely.

What makes a good accountability partner?

Accountability partner selection can make or break your success. It is tempting and easy to ask your best friend, a brother, father, and wife to be that person that you will count on when you are in crisis. But best practices tell us that what never works for many people seldom works for all people, but what always works for many people will usually work for all people.

The most important first consideration is, the best accountability partner is not supposed to be your friend, he is your external accountability. Think parole officer if you must, but this is the person who has the power to come at you hard, expect you to respond, and have power to act decisively in your best interest. So, chose your accountability partner from someone who has himself overcome the same or remarkably similar issue that you are battling, and has the following attributes:

- Someone you will listen to and respect.
- Someone who is not afraid to use their power to command action from you if needed.
- Someone who is not willing to take you only at your word, but who will insist on verification.
- Someone you will give permission to so he can speak freely into your life.
- Someone you are not likely to argue with or manipulate easily.

Start by naming three people you know that would make a good accountability partner. Do not worry about IF they are willing, just name ones that would be good for you.

_____   _____   _____

The Accountability Agreement

Now it is time to draft your accountability agreement (in rough form) so that you can establish what you will ask of your accountability partners, and what you will commit to doing for your own growth.

1. **Write a preamble** to an accountability agreement that you can propose to your partners. They will help you create the final agreement. This preamble should be personalized so that you can ask them for help and give them enough information about the issue without creating a lengthy conversation. If you are not sure how to draft this

preamble, ask your group facilitator or your coach to help you.

Example:

Over the years I have developed a porn addiction/habit that is threatening my marriage. I need help. I am working through a program to help me break free. But to be successful, I need some men who will help me stay strong and be willing to confront me, redirect me, and if needed, beat me up a bit so that I stay strong and on target. I would like to ask you to be that person and invite your intervention and give you authority to speak into my life as you see fit....

2. **Draft the (minimum) actions** YOU will follow in accountability. Include the following:
   - Agree to allow your accountability partner(s) to have contact information on the other stakeholders in your battle to overcome.
   - Agree to a certain level of check-in that YOU will initiate. E.g., weekly conversation, daily text awareness focus, group attendance confirmation, counseling attendance confirmation, etc.
   - Agree to share responsibility to know your cycle and plan so that he can hold you to it if you struggle or fail.
   - Agree that if you violate your accountability, he can call your support network.
   - Agree what will happen if you lapse or relapse, e.g., you will call/text him that you are in trouble immediately.
   - If you relapse you will call him within X hours.
   - You will discuss all relapses within 24 hours, including a plan on how to inform your spouse/fiancé/girlfriend, etc.
   - You will contact her within 48 hours of the relapse, to give you time to settle and plan, but not to cause her to

have to shift and redefine excessive life event history in light of the new DISCOVERY.

3. **Review your proposed agreement** with one of the group coaches and revise as needed. Once you have finalized it and your coach agrees, look at your list of three names again. Will they be good choices? If not, revise the list.

4. **Once you have your final three names**, go to each person individually, in person if possible, and read them the preamble, give them your accountability plan, and ask them to be your partner.

5. **If one says no, go to the next**. Add people if you need to. Keep searching until you have two at least, three is better. If you cannot get at least two, ask your coach to connect you with some of the other men from the program or church who will agree to be your partner. Who knows, your coach may be one of them.

It's All Out WAR!

Introduction to Warfare

In parts of this study, we will use the language of warfare and the language of relationship to frame and guide the individual journey that each man faces as he progresses to victory over his bondage to his process addiction. The connection between warfare and relationship will become obvious as you progress on your journey. For now, let us establish the nature of the war that must be fought.

> *One evening, a wise old Cherokee told his grandson about a battle, one that goes on inside every man. He said, "My son, the battle inside is between two wolves that live in all of us. One is evil; it is anger, envy, jealousy, sorrow, regret, greed, arrogance, self-pity, guilt, resentment, inferiority, lies, false pride, superiority, and ego. The other is good: It is love, joy, peace, hope, serenity, humility, kindness, benevolence, empathy, generosity, truth, compassion, and faith."*

The grandson thought about this for a minute, and then asked his grandfather, "Which wolf wins?"

The wise old Cherokee replied, "Simple, the one that you feed."

You might be thinking, "What does an old parable have to do with my battle with pornography?" The answer is clear. You have a sin nature you were born with—the evil wolf, and you can have the Holy Spirit inside of you—the good wolf. Which one wins out is the one you feed, either by giving into your mental fusions of addiction to pornography or by fleeing evil of all sorts and staying in the Word of God and prayer. Every man, woman, and child in history has had these two forces pulling them throughout their lives. The evil wolf is your enemy and while it is debatable whether you can ever actually kill it, you can certainly kill its food supply which will make it a weak animal and thus not an overpowering threat. C.S. Lewis said it best.

"Lust is a poor, weak, whimpering whispering thing compared with that richness and energy of desire which will arise when lust has been killed."

The enemy is your focus of attack. It should become your first focus. While this seems obvious, most of the time you will notice that you and your fellow warriors will be attacking anything and everything except the enemy. This is due in large part because most people fail to identify who the enemy is. To help you remember exactly who your enemy is, we will refer to your enemy as the **Hated Enemy**.

This simple addition of an adjective (hated) stirs up an emotional response. When you are at risk of misfiring at the wrong person or event, recalling if they are *hated* or not will shock you back into focus. The best example is when you and your spouse are arguing over your behavior. If you attack her by defending yourself or your actions, you are substituting her for the *Hated Enemy* and attacking her. If can recall the *hated enemy* perspective in the moment, you are more likely to back off and correct your aim.

The second focus in warfare must be to preserve or to win over the innocent people who are being affected by your choices of behavior. In other words, to *win the peace* while defeating the enemy.

All relationships are an expression, a communication, a presentation of how you see or value people and your connection to them. Relationships are vital, and specific ones are essential. How you affect those around you in life establishes or destroys those relationships. If you are in a war, and carelessly or heartlessly cause damage to the innocents, you will not be well received. Winning a war also means winning the peace. You begin winning and losing the war and the peace from the very beginning as you simultaneously fight this war on multiple fronts and shield the innocents. How you do this is a matter of tactics. The goal is the same; to win the war and win the peace. You will do this one battle at a time, and you must have effective strategies to know what to do in the moment.

Robert Green[3] authored *The 33 Strategies of War*. This book is described by Greene as *a guide to military principles of war as applied to everyday life*. His study of battles across world history identifies and defines effective strategies to defeat an enemy. Using many of these strategies and principles of warfare, winning life can become just as effective. We will be using some of these strategies, in variation, to fight your personal war against your own *Hated Enemy*. We will also use strategic understanding to win the peace.

A Different Kind of War.

To achieve your purpose of a lifetime defeat of porn addiction, or any other arch villain in your life, you need to learn the art of warfare. Not the military sort of warfare, but the spiritually attuned type of warfare, the same strategy that we see so many great men of the Bible apply to their own lives. Warfare in this sense is knowing who the enemy is, and how to defeat him, while being the one in control of your own outcomes.

We will begin our lessons in warfare with self-direction to establish which relationships are going to be paramount in life for you. To support our dual-focus approach to winning the war and the peace, I will be adding relationship strategies to the war strategies along the way. Remember, you must fight on both fronts, but you must also apply the correct strategies to both.

As we proceed, we will try to separate these concepts by discussing warfare in *military* terms, and peace in *relational* terms. It is important to keep them in the right perspective. With that in mind, let us get started…

Self-Directed Warfare

Begin With the End in Mind. (Stephen R. Cove)[4]

In the war for life, your battles against porn addiction, sex addiction, or cyber-sexual abuse are very personal. The war for control over such addictive behavior in your life reaches far beyond you as an individual. Many of the men who come to me asking for help are there because of a discovery event that has upended their life. The most common catalyst is when a spouse or partner finds the evidence of porn use or cyber-sexual activity, often for the first time, and demands he gets help. Repeated discoveries amplify the pain, and they demand more aggressively that he get this under control. Sometimes marriages are at risk, other times shame and self-loathing are the reason. Regardless of why you are choosing to participate in this process of becoming recovered, there is little doubt in my mind that there are other stakeholders beside yourself.

Collateral damage in warfare is defined as the killing or wounding of civilians and innocents, or other damage that is incidental to the activities of war. In real war, people die who should not die. Property is destroyed that is not a legitimate target, and the region in which the war takes place is impacted by the mere presence of warfare. When you choose to act out by using porn there will be damage, a lot of which will be collateral to the events. This is not easy to accept, but your choice affects others beyond yourself, and in the end, there is no one to blame but you.

It is because you have *chosen* to engage in an activity that indulges self at the expense of your own character and at the expense of others in your life. You are now struggling to undo whatever damage has resulted. For this reason, we must begin with *you* in our quest to defeat porn and its allies for good. We begin with *self-directed* warfare.

You will need time to prepare to wage war on your own mind in order to bring the enemy to its knees and save the innocent victims for more harm. Like all warfare, you will want to develop strategies to defeat the enemy. To be effective, you must "get your head in the game." Or more specifically, to rescue your mind from being captive to the enemy and reengage your personal agency to be mindful once more. It's all about getting your head in the game. Throughout this group process, Greene's take on warfare will help define some effective strategies to intentionally understand and pursue the *Hated Enemy*.

Declaring War on the Enemy

Throughout your life, you will fight many battles. Not all of those battles will be defining ones. Many should never be fought at all. Some must be fought. Many will be vital, demanding that you never underestimate their importance.

This first strategy demands two things from you as a warrior. First, you must know the cause you are fighting for. Then you must define who or what threatens that cause. This will tell you who the real enemy is, and this is who (or what) you must fight. Greene names this struggle the *Polarity Strategy*. Knowing which battles *must be fought*, and who the *true enemy* is. This sounds simple. But simple is not always easy.

Who is the enemy? If you assumed porn is the enemy, you would be mistaken. Porn is not a person or entity that has the will or the means to interfere in your life's path. Porn is not what threatens your quest or your just cause. No, you cannot simply declare war on porn. You cannot even control porn. It is out there. It is everywhere. And it is beyond your ability to defeat. It is part of the world we live in, and it is toxic to all men. It can result in major destruction in the lives of those who come into contact with it. But porn is not a free agent that can attack you. No, the enemy is not porn. That is too simple.

The enemy is closer to home. The enemy is *your* own mind. What you must begin to see, as you look at life through the scope of your weapon, are the *processes* of your own mind that have interfered with your personal agency, your control of your own self. Porn is just one outcome of a mind that has been hijacked. In spiritual terms, we call this *sin*.

Greene tells us that to smoke out the true enemy, you must learn to identify the patterns and signs that point him out. To declare war, you must know who or what you are fighting. In cyber-sexual abuse or addiction, the true *Hated Enemy* resides *in* your mind. It is an alliance between certain factions that come together to take control of your life. These factions are not infiltrators, they are insurgents, traitors, turncoats. That's right, there is a rebellion in your own mind that is in revolt against the natural order of the authority of your life—you! It is indeed the battle of the two wolves.

You are created as a free agent with free will. But you are intended to follow a course of maximum outcome and potential. God has created you with all the capacity to live life in fullness and power. That same potential is what we see in the life of Christ as He effectively walked in full knowledge of His own person and purpose. We are created to do the same, but we sell off bits and pieces of our divine inheritance as we stumble through life. Like Jacob's brother Esau, we sell our birthright for a bowl of stew, or in this case, porn.

This comes slowly and by progression. Think about how you developed as a young man. How your thoughts developed into a line of belief, your philosophical point of view that informs your most heart-felt opinions. Such things do not just spring up overnight. The same is true with your sexual perspective or your way of seeing relationships. Over time you gather experiences, and then, as the enormity of those experiences begins to coalesce into an identity, you take on certain thoughts leading to your feelings and actions. Over time, you alter your *love map*, and naturally, your journey is corrupted. Where sin is a specific act or action taken, sinfulness is a state of being, a habitual practice of action, an addiction to a choice.

Porn addiction works by the same rules. You see first see some porn when you are eleven or twelve years old. At that time, it is exciting because you are getting an insider's peek into the adult world. Sex and sexuality are mysterious to a child, but a topic of endless speculation. Seeing pornography immerses the young mind into a new level of exposure. Unfortunately, at that age, the average male is not ready to absorb the meaning and affective power of porn imagery. Only the excitement is recognized. And with excitement comes dopamine. That wonderful feel-good brain drug that rewards you in a way nothing else ever could. The attraction is set. You want more.

At this point, it is not really even about sex. It is about excitement, curiosity, adventure, and of course experiencing the forbidden. But when you eat forbidden fruit, there is going to be a consequence. As with the original eating from the wrong tree, there was an awakening that altered the very essence of the mind of two young people. "Then the eyes of both of them were opened, and they realized they were naked…" Genesis 3:7. The consequence of disobedience and choosing to disregard God's plan and instruction was the beginning of a new *pattern* of thought and action for Adam and Eve. In the same way, when a young man samples the forbidden fruit, he is not prepared for what he discovers. The flood of experience will set up new and powerful pathways in his mind that will take him to a place where just moments ago he was not craving. This path progresses with repetition, hijacking one function of mind and soul after another, until porn and addiction are in control as surely as death and sin took the human race in the Garden of Eden.

Later we will talk about the power of mental fusions, or neural pathways, and how they function in addiction and life choices. But for now, let us move forward with the understanding that the *Hated Enemy* lives inside your mind, and it is there that most of the meaningful battles must be fought.

You Cannot Fight the Past

Presence-of-Mind. You cannot war on the past and win any victories that matter. Do not fall for this false battle. In the War of the Mind[5] strategy, you must keep present. Presence of mind allows you to focus on what you can fight, on what you can change. When you wage war on the mind, you fight the constant accusations of the past. This smoke screen of shame and habit blocks your victory. Instead, you must move forward, take control of the present, and apply the past as a tool, not a focus.

47

"The past is already written. The ink is dry." That now famous line from Game of Thrones[6] says it all. You cannot wage war on the past and win any victories that matter. Do not fall for this false battle against the past, defending your actions that have already been chosen and acted out. In the war of the mind strategy[7] you must keep in the present. The **presence of mind** allows you to focus on what you can fight-what you can change. When you wage war on the mind, you fight the **constant accusations of the past**.as a distraction from the present, not as the actual enemy. The past creates a smoke screen of shame and habit which blocks your victory by causing you to fight something that is already decided. Instead, you must move forward, take control of the present, and apply the past as a tool of wisdom, not as focus a focus of battle.

Letting the past govern your life or relationships is a flawed strategy based on the notion that by holding onto the past, its pain, or grievances, you can force others to change and treat you differently, or by keeping your anger alive, it will defend you against future hurt. Such actions trap and limit your present focus to the past. In doing so your future will be doomed by the past and extend your suffering. There is no benefit to lingering in pain.

This bitterness is anger combined with grief, festering inside of you. It distorts your thinking to the extent that your character and life choices become unhealthy. Instead of healing, bitterness allows unforgiveness to take root in your heart, emphasizing a record of wrongs (1 Cor: 13), and driving aggressive or destructive reactions toward people and events.

Below I have illustrated various *Presence of Mind* Strategies commonly applied, to help you comprehend the traps that exist in each. I have also illustrated a balanced approach that will help you combat those traps. If you have already fallen into one of the more harmful patterns, escaping it can be challenging. However, well applied introspection can bring decisive change and lift you out of these hidden traps. In helping clients learn to do life free of the past I usually start by using a simile. My favorite is to imagine that life is like driving a car.

Imagine yourself driving a car. You are behind the wheel and in control. What you do moment by moment determines where you will end up in the near and the far future. You are navigating towards a goal. In the car you are present in the moment with the controls. You are observing the dashboard and your speed, you are aware of the amount of gas you have, whether or not any indicator lights have come on, or if any gauges are indicating problems. You are aware of the people in your car, and of the cars nearby, of where the lines are on the road, and what the road conditions are like. This is all *presence of mind*. You are present with your driving.

In your car, there is a rear-view mirror, and side view mirrors. These tell you what has just taken place and what is behind you. They give you a brief but necessary view of anything in the past that could be causing you present or future harm. You see bad drivers speeding up behind you, overtaking you, or passing you. You see erratic behavior. You see lights on emergency vehicles approaching. This rearward view is important, even though for the most part, what you see in those mirrors is the past. Sometimes, the past catches up with you, overtakes you and causes you problems.

You also have a windshield. Through this windshield you see what is coming in front of you. You are able to see ahead far enough to make decisions in the moment about where you want to be in the future. Part of that future is the *near future*, perhaps the next quarter mile. Sometimes it is even a matter of a few hundred yards. There are also signs that you see in the windshield indicating what is coming up ahead, what your route needs to be in the next few miles, with mile markers that tell you where you are presently so you can make plans. This is your future view.

There is a reason the windshield is larger than your rear-view mirror. What is in front of you is a whole lot more important to your well-being than what is behind you. The same is true with your side view windows. What is next to you is more important than what is behind you, which is why we design cars with a sweeping view of the present around us.

To successfully navigate your vehicle and get where you want to go safely you need to have all three of these views in mind. This means that you are present in your car and in control, taking into consideration what is behind you as necessary but within perspective, and focusing very carefully on what is ahead of you so you can make good plans in the present moment. This is a past-present-future focus. This is wisdom in action. Taking in the information and prioritizing that information to make you safe.

If we were to drive our cars the way we navigate and drive our lives, we would end up dead. This is because we tend to focus too much on one or two aspects of this three-dimensional view. If we have experienced deep hurt in the past, we tend to focus on the past. This would be like driving your car staring at the rearview mirror. It will not take long before you run off the road or hit something. Others spend all their time in the present looking around them for choices they get to make, like checking their phone, rolling down the windows or eating food. If someone is only immediately present, they cannot make plans for the future, nor can they see danger coming from the rear. Some drivers are casual in their collective presence of mind, acting almost like passengers, focusing more on looking out the windows at the scenery, without any thought or presence of mind about what they need to be doing with that information. No, if we drove our cars the way we manage our lives we would be dead.

So, what can we do about this? The answer lies in keeping a three-dimensional awareness which views all three dimensions in proportion, looking at the diverse ways in which our awareness can go out of proportion, or even become myopic. Below I will describe each of the major ways that people deal with the presence of mind and the trap of dysfunction in them. Then, we will discuss a view that focuses on healthful presence of mind, so that those who are struggling with the hurts of the past, difficulties in the present, and fear of the future can learn to function. We start first with the most common form of presence of mind when damage, hurt, or transgression defines your life; a life lived in the past.

Past-Present Focus. Past-present living occurs whenever the past is the primary focus in daily life. The present is determined by the past, freezing the individual into living out grief and trauma from the past in each moment of the present. How the present is lived out sets up the factors that then influence the unwritten future. When your past is too powerful, due to pain or habit, your present becomes anchored to the past. Your present is defined by the past. Your present is controlled by the past. Your present *is* the past. You are stuck in the past like a dog tied to a post, you can only progress so far before you are yanked back by the collar around your throat.

Think about how the past and its accusations limit your present. "*If only...*" This simple sentence stem can trigger enormous negativity and regret.

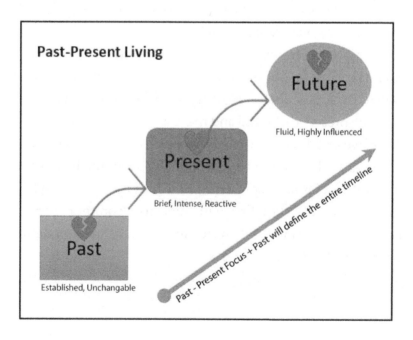

Past-Present Living

Future
Fluid, Highly Influenced

Present
Brief, Intense, Reactive

Past
Established, Unchangable

Past - Present Focus + Past will define the entire timeline

Present-only Focus. Many would say, "live in the moment, it is all you have." Sounds nice, but that is dangerous. Present only living occurs when the focus is only on the moment. Live in the moment ignores the influences of the past or accepts it, then defines the moment as all that matters. This *taking care of number one* attitude ignores consequences and justifies all choices. The future is now held hostage to the happenstance of a multitude of moments as the past blurs into an unfocused March towards a self-created fate. The present is continually active and constantly changing. Like a flood of water, it can take you anywhere. You need banks and shores to contain the flood and keep it safe. When someone tries to live only for the present, they become amazingly comfortable in the moment, disregarding containment. This leads to consequences that could be avoided. Your use of porn or cybersex is one potent example. In the moment there is the pleasure, stress relief,

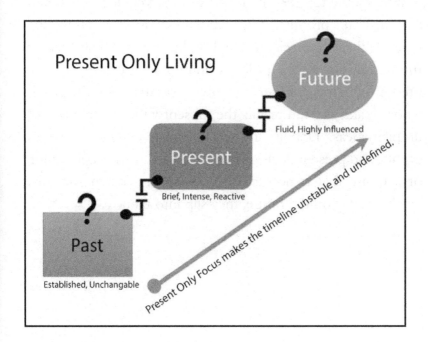

excitement—whatever it is you crave. But the consequences are far-reaching and long lasting.

Since the past allows us to benefit from insight through consequences, good and bad, the past becomes the containment or boundaries that we need to channel the flood of the present into a safe and healthy direction. Yet, those who live only in the moment ignore the past, fail to take heed of past lessons, allow repeated failures to creep into their decisions, altering their potential outcomes. Character, as we have defined it, is that outward expression of the inward process. The habits of the moment, especially living only in the moment, create that unreliable, selfish, and heedless character that others find repulsive.

Future-only Focus. So, what about the future, if the past is set, and the present is uninformed, then how does someone move into the future? The future is a marvelous place, full of potential and promise. You naturally envision a future, and typically that is a special future. But, having a singular focus, a future-only focus, is equally as limiting as a past-present or present-only focus. Future only living occurs when the past is ignored, and the future fills the present with assumptions of utopian ideas. Lost is any wisdom that comes from past events, and present decisions are all driven by the assumption of a future that is not actually written yet. When someone dwells mostly on the future, they slip into fantasy.

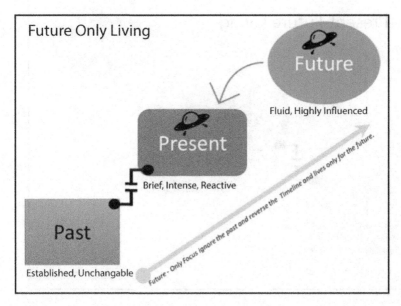

Fantasy is fun, and visions for a special future are motivating. Many great people have been propelled by a strong future goal. But there is a catch. You cannot live *in* the future. The future has yet to become real, and you never really arrive. You are stuck existing in the present, no matter how hard you wish for the future.

Present-future Focus. Present future living uses the hope and possibility of the future to help make worthy choices in the present, looking forward to setting up possibilities for a better future. For most of my clients, my efforts end up teaching present-future focusing. It is generally enough to help them see how the future can inspire, creating a level of healthy anxiety, a healthy dissatisfaction for standing still. It inspires progression. Like the rope that ties past dwellers to their past, present-future visionaries are bound to the future, not by a rope, but by an invisible force not unlike a massive rubber

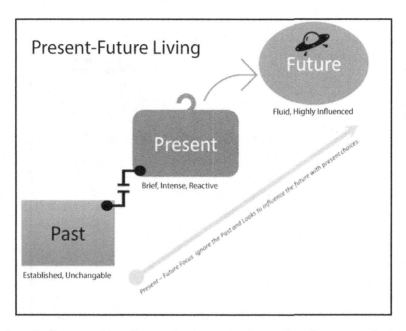

band. It stretches from the present into the future and the energy contained in that stretch provides momentum to move forward with a strong purpose.

The term used in the world of motivational theory is *creative tension* coined by Peter Senge[8]. The energy or "tension" of the stretch to the future is that rubber band that connects the two. This focus allows for real change by defining the gap between where you are and where you would like to be. That is the *momentum* we want to use in recovery.

As you can see none of these presence of mind strategies truly allows you to live a whole and functional life. The presence of mind requires a bit more. Below is the best way to live, if life were like driving a car.

Wisdom Focus

In 12-step groups, the members often cite the Serenity prayer at the end of the meeting.

> *God, grant me the serenity to accept the things I cannot change, courage to change the things I can, and wisdom to know the difference.*

Wisdom is a combination of past, present, and future, which is why it is seen most powerfully in older people. Wisdom brings to a present-future focus visionary some essential guidance from the past. In our water analogy, the flood that must be contained can be random, like a lake where all the water just happens to drain into the lowest area. This is happenstance. Events that just settle themselves without purpose or guidance beyond the natural. But if you apply wisdom, such as recalling the past when a flood devastated a town, you can plan a vision for the future and channel flood waters towards a defined outcome. The future motivates, the past informs, and all happens in the present. The present channeled to purpose is the flood waters contained by two banks, the past which is *wisdom* from experience, and the future which are *consequences and goals*.

If life is like driving a car, then wisdom is paying attention to all the data input, proportional to their ability to impact you now, in into the future. You pay attention to the *here-and-now* details of your vehicle, your speed, and your fuel, as well as to the drivers around you. You keep between the lines and are responsive to any sudden changes. You also take a glance back periodically to make sure nothing is coming up that needs you to make some adjustments. And most of all, you focus on the immediate future of what is in front of you, while keeping in mind the long view of where you are going. Life is just like driving a car, it takes practice, attentiveness, and wisdom to know how to respond when things change.

In our car once more, the wise driver is the experienced driver. He is present with the activity of operating the vehicle, aware of what has passed that could require some action, aware of the future and its demands as well as promises, and gathers all of this input into the choices he makes moment by moment

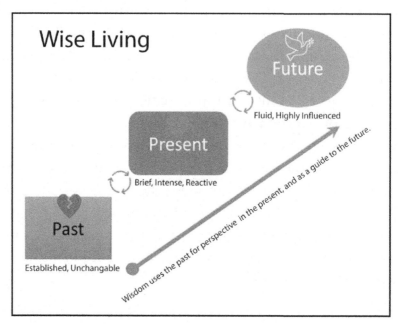

in the present. He is engaged in the full awareness of driving. Life lived in full awareness and engagement means choices are made in the moment that support the future with wisdom, having learned from the past.

Trying to live in the past is like trying to drive a car with your attention primarily focused on the rear-view mirror. In a car, you are in three states at one time; you are observant of the past, what's behind you, you are focused on the future, what's ahead of you, but you operate in the present, the act of operating the car. If you spend most of your attention on the rearview mirror, you will not see what's coming, and your present choices in driving will go wrong, and you will be in danger of disaster.

Counterbalance Strategy

To apply a war of the mind strategy, you must know what happens when things are wrongly executed. The risk of an unfocused present causes unexpected consequences to your mission and muddles your defined goal(s) for the future. Green reminds us that while not allowing the past to become the battle ground, a *Counterbalance Strategy* is required so that neither the present nor the future takes over completely. Wisdom integrates all three views, past, present, and future.

Sense of Urgency

Immediate circumstances cannot be allowed to distract you from presence of mind. Adversity comes in many forms, often from where you would wish you could find an ally. If your spouse is feeling triggered by her own feelings, you will no doubt find distraction from your presence of mind strategy and begin to battle her. Many men have prolonged their relationship healing from this one avoidable mistake. Some have even lost the war to these battles. We will tackle that in the near future, but for now, keep the counterbalance by detaching yourself from the insertion of chaos. The fog of war can cause the most well-intentioned warrior to make deadly errors of judgment.

Death Ground Perspective

Future only focus is a waste of time and creates a different enemy. Wasting time daydreaming of the future, instead of engaging in the present with all its potential roadblocks to the future, limits forward progress as surely as failure to cut the ties of the past holds you in place. A death ground happens when you are in a place where it is fight or die. Death grounds compel you to fight! No complacency is allowed. You must proceed with the fight, grow, struggle, and overcome the challenges, or die in place. In valorous living, self-leadership is demanded, and your focus must be on the COMMITMENT you have made to yourself, and to others, to make the changes needed to make everyone safe. It's a do or die commitment that counts.

Team Warfare

Without relationships, plans, tactics, and skills make no difference. The following tactics are chosen to help you build a *conjoint perspective*, to keep the relationship intact, even healthy, while fighting the *Hated Enemy*.

The problem of solitary leadership is that individuals in any relationship or group have their own points of view, their own priorities, and their own agendas. Leadership and participation are not about forcing people into one singular opinion. It is about casting a vision that others can buy into, that would include their needs and vision, but are also supportive of the collective vision. Leadership means focusing on what makes for a great outcome, not what any one individual wants.

But there is a catch. If any one person in the marriage, family, or organization pressures others to meet only their needs, or to attend solely to their point of view, pain, or expectation, that pressure can lead to groupthink. **Groupthink** is a form of consensus. It occurs when a group (including a married couple) sets aside personal beliefs, needs, or other thoughts, in favor of the group. This is often caused by a highly persuasive individual or cohort of persons who leverage a point of view into acceptance.

When group thinking occurs, individual perspective is suppressed or even lost. This can be dangerous since the setting aside of personal beliefs can result in some less than optimal, one-sided decisions. The need to appease the group or placate the most insistent or powerful person or faction can limit cognitive complexity. Without complexity, myopic or narrow views prevail, opening the outcome to an imbalance of power, health, or the needs of the individuals.

Groupthink is often the result of being well-intentioned, but more often leads to irrational decisions. For instance, when a betrayed spouse is struggling with internalized pain of betrayal, she or he may demand retribution on an ongoing basis. In an attempt to appease demands for healing the betrayed, the person responsible for causing the betrayal may become so self-effacing that they lose the ability to overcome shame, resulting in a loss of self-esteem. For males, when self-esteem comes under threat, the fight of flight system activates automatically, resulting in high levels of defensiveness and resistance.

Groupthink causes the individual to value consensus over logic or reason. Groupthink ignores critical data to stay in consensus, which can lead to major unintended consequences. Participation in the team effort should be collaborative and participating, but not irrationally constrained from sharing or influencing the outcomes or decisions. Mission drift can be directly influenced by groupthink. Remember, the mission should not focus only on the momentary battle at hand, there is a higher goal; win the war and win the peace!

Segment Your Forces: Control Chaos

Chaos happens despite planning. That is the nature of chaos—it cannot be planned away. To control chaos, you must be able to segment your forces (you, your spouse, your collective team, etc.) into independent actions. There are many actions that must be undertaken to manage the intrusion of cyber-sexual abuse or addiction in a relationship.

While you are working on sobriety by applying self-control, your spouse is working on *betrayal trauma*. You are both working on relationship maintenance. You will be working on empathic attending. She will also be working on awareness and emotional or cognitive restructuring. You will both be working on forgiveness. In segmenting forces, and controlling chaos, you must recognize what battle you are in *at the moment*, who owns the problem, and which team or person is tasked with action.

Who Owns the problem?

Blaming and arguing are problematic in any relationship. Often the solution is found in knowing who owns this problem. This can reduce the impact or leverage of blame shift and guilt. There are several ways to determine ownership.

Who has the power to fix this problem? Problems belong (most often) to the person who can best solve them. If your wife is upset because your search history has been erased, which triggered her fear, she will confront you. There are immediately two problems here:

1. You made a choice to remove the search history and triggered her fear.

2. She is now upset because her fear is activated.

Problem number 1, the activating problem, belongs to you. You made the choice to erase history. That choice was an active violation of your understanding about corrective accountability. Or, at least, it indicates that you were choosing to do something selfishly without considering the impact on her. Since only you can control you, only you can choose not to erase your history. You own the problem.

However, problem number 2 remains. She is still triggered and upset. This takes us to the next test of *who owns the problem.*

"Who is actually upset about this problem?" If the problem is upsetting *you*, then it belongs to you. For instance, if you feel shame about your past behavior, and your spouse confronts you about a violation of your accountability or other behavior, your shame will trigger, and you will get upset (become defensive) because you feel shame. The problem is not what she said or what she did. The problem is your unresolved shame. You own this problem.

"Is this problem a shared problem?" Sometimes we can be upset about a problem that someone else has caused, or events force us to resolve. An example would be a suspension from work after being discovered using porn on company devices or time. You have a problem because your employer has chosen to discipline your behavioral choices. But your wife shares the problem because it is causing emotional disruption to the marriage, triggers her fears, and may be placing a financial burden on the family. There are several problems here, but they are shared because neither one of you can solve them on your own. It will take two of you to bring about a resolution to the impact on your marriage.

The Problems of Ownership

Problem number 2. Despite the conflict that has developed in your relationship due to your specific betraying activity, you are unlikely to be responsible for all the problems that your spouse will assign to you. Problem ownership tells you how to respond. If you own it, you must accept ownership and solve it yourself, then offer support for any collateral damages you forced onto your spouse or others. If it was forced upon you, but is not your problem, you likely need to express your boundary with effective response tactics to give the problem back to the owner. If it is shared, then you can use effective communication strategies (I-messages, empathetic attending, etc.) to listen, attend, and repair empathic failures or behaviors.

The focus for adapting to chaos is to be confident in your decision-making accuracy so that you can make decisions quickly, but not make bad ones. By segmenting your forces into responsibilities for action, your collective mission will be better accomplished.

Transform Your War Into a Crusade

Here is the most important strategy you can learn in repairing the relationship and winning the peace while simultaneously fighting the war on the *Hated Enemy*. Recast the war into a crusade. A crusade has the benefit of being a moral imperative; something you both want to achieve. Crusades demand personal commitment to a higher ideal. Crusades become life-altering.

Up until now, if you are like most couples, the pain, anger, and shame that divides you creates a mis-focus. Standing face to face, you confront, defend, and attack towards each other. This happens because for each of you, the other is the trigger of strong emotions. So, you naturally want to stop the pain and force the other into submission. But this is like a circular firing squad. While you aim for the center, everyone in the circle is included in the target. You must learn that in your crusade, you must stand shoulder-to-shoulder against the *Hated Enemy*, so you shoot at it, never face-to-face where your marriage is in the crossfire.

To create a crusade, it is necessary for all stakeholders to be more concerned about maintaining the higher moral or relational outcome of the marriage than their immediate concern for self. To focus on the marriage, not the persons. We see this type of *crusade energy* in new parents as they shift from being a *self-indulgent couple* to becoming a completely sacrificial *parenting team* once a new baby arrives in the family. Giving up sleep, privacy, individual wants and needs, all focusing on the needs of the baby, is a crusade that must be maintained without fail.

When you, your spouse, family, and accountability partners join in a crusade against the *Hated Enemy,* individual survival and restoration shift from the transient need of the person as the primary concern, into at focus on the success of the entire team in recovering the marriage and family.

Now that you have an idea what warfare means in your personal quest against porn and cybersexual addiction, it is time to begin building a strategy. If you are working through the Renewed Mind Workbook, this will be covered in detail in weeks two and three.

(ISBN: 979-8989238620, https://a.co/d/0MW8FWZ on amazon),

A Warrior's Objective

This section next section is duplicated as an exercise in the Renewed Mind Workbook, week two, for those in group or working through the materials in the proscribed program. If you do not have the workbook, I encourage you to get a copy now on Amazon, (ISBN: 979-8-9892386-2-0), so that you can develop your own war plan and relationship recovery in depth.

The Act of War: Consider how to answer the following.

1. **Your choices:** Consider both the choices that you discovered so far, plus the choices you make now about your addiction and those affected by your addiction, as well as what you choose to give up or maintain so that your addiction can continue.
2. **Discovery.** A discovery event is often triggered when your spouse, employer, or others discover your porn use, or when you come to a vivid realization that you are under the spell of porn and cannot break free. Describe your most potent discovery moment.
3. **Collateral damages** occur when personal actions affect others in orbit around your life. Stop now and consider all the people and ways that collateral damage is being done because of your choices. Name the people, name the damages.
4. Now ask yourself, "why am I doing this recovery program?" Describe the *for who, for what*, or the *why* of your reasons.

The Polarity Strategy:

Get your head in the game and begin to build your strategy of war by addressing the following:

- What is your "cause" your "crusade"?

- What are the threats to your victory?
- What exposures impact your beliefs, thoughts, etc.?
- What are the mind games that keep your addiction possible?
- What are your triggers? E.g., your own selfishness, life conflicts, interaction with other or specific people, other events.
- What are the emotions that result from your triggering?
- What strategies do you use or deploy to make those emotions less unpleasant?
- What habits have you developed to mitigate your discomfort and allow your strategies to happen?
- What visible routines have resulted from your habits that let your true addictive character leak out?
- What from the above list determines the outcomes in your life that you do not like?
- Based on the points you have just explored, who or what are the factions that are actively engaged in a war against you?
- Who or what is the true *Hated Enemy* that you must declare war on?

Name your *Hated Enemy*.

_____

Stop Fighting the Past, it's Established.

Being present is more than just the present...

The natural order in your life has become damaged. Consider the previous lesson on how the past is formed and then how it informs the present and the future. Use this to examine your own development of self to determine how it affected you in the following ways:

- In your **Young Mind**
- How it affected your **Developmental Hurdles**
- How it set up **Reinforcements**
- The specific outcomes from your **Exposures**

There once was a man who was addicted to cigarettes. A concerned friend confronted him one day and asked, "Don't you know those things are going to kill you?" The smoker answered, "Yes" but proceeded to light up anyway.

The point to this story is that while we may recognize the long-term risk of behavior, including the likelihood of an ugly death, because that behavior has not killed us *yet*, we ignore reality and are likely to engage in it anyway. Afterall, the future seems far off. *Yet* is a powerful word. It can produce or dispel thinking errors. In this case, *yet* blocks the inevitability of a future since it is unlikely to happen now, so pleasure can override fear.

Risk Versus Reward:

- What is at risk when you use cybersex?
- What are the consequences of setbacks or mistakes in your management of your sobriety?
- What is the eventual consequence of failure?
- Can you predetermine when you will cross that line?
- What is allowing you to risk coming close to that line?

Urgency: Staying on Mission is Vital.

- What distractions are common in your life that take your head out of the game?
- What adversities compete for your sobriety?
- Who is most likely to distract you, why, and how?
- What is most likely to distract you, why, and how?
- What can/should/will you do to stay on mission?

Willpower:

If anyone ever told you they were porn or cybersexually addicted but chose to quit and *did it on their own*, they are lying, minimizing, or never were addicted to begin with. Perhaps they are in denial, and their addiction is still there, just temporarily under control. Even those who have told me that they prayed their addiction away and God healed them eventually relapse when the pressure is great enough. The truth is, it is nearly impossible for a porn addict to fully quit once and for all without some very specific help. As a Christian who does indeed believe in miracles and healing, I also believe that God seldom provides miraculous deliverance over our chosen behaviors. It is unlikely that God will usurp someone's free will decisions. So, please accept that *recovery* from porn is not likely to be cured through miraculous intervention, nor is it an individually empowered act.

Here is why:

- Dopamine craving keeps you tied to your addiction. You are under its direct control.
- It demands that you do what it wants to keep the dopamine flowing or you will be punished with withdrawal, anxiety, and cravings.

- It promises you that if you feed it, it will reward you, and it has the power to do just that.
- Breaking the dopamine connection requires something bigger and stronger to motivate you to change.

John Maxwell put it this way, *"People change when they hurt enough that they have to change, learn enough that they want to change, receive enough that they are able to change."*

Now, be honest and ask yourself:

- Have I hurt enough yet? How much more pain will I choose to suffer and cause?
- Have I learned enough? What am I willing to do to learn what it takes, and then apply it?
- Am I receiving enough support and guidance to be able to? If not, what has been in the way? If I am, why have I not been able to so far?

Winning the Peace

Life is All About Relationships.

How we relate to ourselves is crucial in determining how we relate to others, and how we relate to the world at large. Both intra-personal and inter-personal battles of life occur every day. Over time, the smaller and greater wins and losses aggregate to determine how we view life and then set in motion many of the outcomes we experience as an individual, which then impacts the quality and nature of our relationships. To engage in life, we have three choices in how we approach these battles. We can be offensive, defensive, or strategic. Much of the time, our choice is based on how we see ourselves in the relationship connected to the battle.

Offensive approaches are connected to preset feelings of being unsafe in the world, and a sense that a strong stance is needed against the assumed and inevitable abuse or control from others. This tends to preemptively go on the defensive in more extreme ways, such as blocking, controlling, judging or over-reactive to even the suggestion of interference or criticism from others. Power and control responses are common with offensive approaches.

Defensive approaches are commonly connected to feelings of insecurity and rejection, being unfairly treated, attacked, judged, or controlled. Reactions here are to defend the self and self-image through blaming, arguing, gaslighting, and withdrawing.

Strategic approaches are informed by considering the past and the present, and looking for a different future outcome that habit has provided so far. This is wisdom. Strategies look to self to uncover the causes of internal conflicts and feelings that are not necessarily the fault or responsibility of others and are within the control of self. Reactions when strategy is used are generally measured, cautious, open, and malleable. Just be careful not to use strategies to manipulate or control others. Strategies should be applied to self.

Do you want to be Offensive, Defensive, or Strategic in your war against porn?

So far in our study we have addressed your personal actions and the need to get your life in control, ready for war, and how to maintain the peace. Now we are going to change focus to those who are the innocent victims of your past (or current) poor choices.

For all human beings, relationship safety is the highest order of need once food and shelter are established. Maslow's famous hierarchy of needs names five strata of needs.

Maslow's Hierarchy of Needs

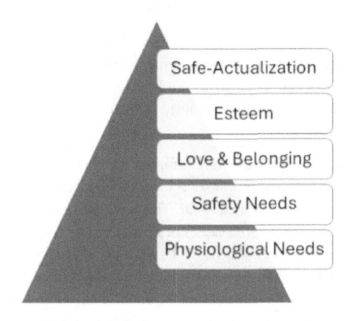

The foundation layer contains the necessary components for survival: air, water, food, shelter, sleep, clothing, and reproduction. Reproduction does not necessarily mean sex as our culture defines it, e.g., as an activity for pleasure. It is essential to the survival of the species, and therefore is a built-in physiological drive. Until foundational needs are satisfied, the rest of Maslow's needs strata are not possible.

The second strata contain the Safety needs. Safety is a much broader category than most assume. Safety can be completely self-managed and created but are also impacted by the environment and those around us.

Third in the hierarchy is love and belonging. This is where family and friends come in. Safety and love/belonging are inter-connected and could be on one stratum. But Maslow's famous hierarchy says they are separate. Look at the list on strata four in Figure 1. Friendship, intimacy, family, sense of connection. Which of these would you subordinate to strata two needs? Many would say that access to property or employment is much less important than a sense of connection and love. The final two strata, esteem and self-actualization are left to work on if you have space in your life after the first three, at least by traditional Maslow thinking.

Intimacy is a Basic Need Too.

As a counselor, I can tell you that I see many more clients who are emotionally or mentally devastated by the loss of connection than by the loss of a job, home, or large sums of money. People matter most to people; we just do not always act like they do. By choosing porn or other cybersexual addiction over people, you cut deeply into this core need for the most important in your life, your spouse, family, friends, and self. You insert porn or internet time between the safety and love/belonging strata in the hierarchy of needs for your own self, and between physiological needs and the safety strata for your spouse. In Maslow's hierarchy, it is presumed that the strata you have not fulfilled is the strata you are stuck in, and this becomes the limiting or minimum factor. You cannot move towards potential until the lower order needs are met.

Liebig's Law of the Minimum

In life you will find that the **Law of the Minimum** controls and confounds your efforts to establish meaningful relationships and success. Liebig (1840) used a barrel to illustrate the principle as developed by Sprengel (1828). The barrel's capacity is limited to the shortest of the staves in that barrel, despite all intentions of the original design. When the design is ignored or altered, a limitation is established.

Minimum

In the case of cyberaddiction, you may find that your lowest stave, which we call the minimum or limiting factor might be self-indulgence, self-love, need for escape, etc. So, when seeking to become restored and healed from cybersexual addiction, you must face the limiting factors first before you can see any true success.

You have many staves in your barrel. Most of your staves have to do with you as an individual: your selfishness, control, need for excitement, character choices, etc. But many are linked to your spouse. In those staves one limiting factor is her unwillingness or inability to move forward as quickly as you want to. In your individual barrel, the health of your primary relationship is a major potential limiting factor. If this stave is too short, you will fall short of most of your goals in life. And, as we have seen in Maslow's hierarchy, most of your self-improvement efforts will not succeed without first attending to this most important stave in the barrel.

Putting first things first, you must understand the nature and limiting factors of her *betrayal trauma* if you have any hope of successfully reactivating the friendship in your marriage.

Betrayal trauma

Betrayal trauma is an unofficial but common term applied to what is clinically known as Complex Post Traumatic Stress Disorder (C-PTSD). We know the signs and the stages of *betrayal trauma* from studies on abused children and abused spouses. But not all abuse that results in *betrayal trauma* is intentional or obvious. That is why most porn users never stop to consider exactly why a spouse is suffering so much from the discovery of their porn use. C-PTSD occurs when a person looks to another for support and safety, and in turn that safe person becomes their abuser or betrayer. This results in a complex form of trauma due to the existential damage to trust and wellbeing. We call this trust and wellbeing *safety*, but it is so much more than that simple word conveys.

Imagine for a moment a small child of eight or less, who loves her parents. One day, the father gets drunk, beats the mom and the child, and then runs from the house. The child will be in shock from this major violation of all that she knows about safety. "If my dad can hurt us like that, then I am no longer safe."

Post-traumatic stress disorder is a state of external trauma that has caused specific dysfunction for more than a month. The criteria are grouped into three areas:

1. Hypervigilance due to a sense of ongoing threat.

2. Avoidance of places, people, events, etc. that trigger anxious arousal.

3. Intrusive thoughts or feelings that cause the person to reexperience the trauma.

Trauma results from exposure to an incident or series of events that are emotionally disturbing or life-threatening with lasting adverse effects on the individual's functioning and mental, physical, social, emotional, and/or spiritual well-being. Now, add to that the alarm that occurs when such an event comes, not from the chances of ordinary life, but at the hands of the person that you count on to keep you safe. This is *complex* PTSD. The threat is not only personal, but it might also be ongoing.

Complex PTSD adds three more critical symptoms:

1. Affect dysregulation.
2. Negative self-concept.
3. Interpersonal/relational disturbance.

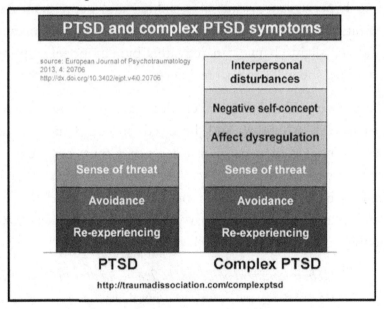

FIGURE 2. CPTSD SYMPTOM CLUSTERS

Let us take these one by one.

Affect dysregulation is the most noticeable symptom. Because the event or discovery cuts deep into the safety of the relationship, a dilemma is created.

"The one I love hurts me—if I stay, I will be hurt again."

"The one I love hurts me—if I leave, I may miss out on regaining his love."

There are a number of these dilemmas, but every betrayed spouse or partner that I have ever spoken to expresses this basic fear. It leaves them in a limbo of indecision. Stay or go? Risk or lose? This is what we call an *ambiguous loss*. A loss with no foreseeable close. Since it is ambiguous, normal coping strategies just will not work, and the victim is left adrenalized into hypervigilance while also sinking into depression. As a result, the fight or flight response center is on fulltime alert, and any slight change can activate a big emotional response. In short, she will begin to feel crazy.

Negative self-worth is the cruelest part of *betrayal trauma*. It leaves the wounded and betrayed spouse believing that somehow it is their fault, or at least they must change to get their guy to stay off porn. Most all women who grew up in our culture have serious doubts about their bodies drilled into their self-concept. When the man cheats, all that insecurity is activated. So now they feel like garbage goods.

> *"If he is looking at porn, does he find me unattractive, unexciting, too something, not enough something? Am I good enough? How can I compete with cybersexual pros?"*

Finally, there is what Figure 2 calls **relational disturbances**. I prefer to call this ***relational distancing***. Either way, the nature of relationship has been damaged for the betrayed spouse. She will have a chain of doubts that nag at her along with her negative self-worth and emotional disruptions. The mental dilemma here looks like this:

> *"Who is this man I thought I knew so well. If he can do this, did I miss something? Is he not who I thought he was? Am I that bad at judging people? If I am, who else have I misjudged? Who else might hurt me? Is the world even truly safe? I need to protect myself."*

This last stream of thought triggers and retriggers all other CPTSD symptoms. The cycle is inescapable it seems, and so her emotional reserves are used up. The only logical action that the betrayed spouse sees is to either ignore it and take him at his word he is changing, or set extreme controls on him, the marriage, and her own life. Some women do both or cycle back and forth between to two. The *betrayal trauma* wound becomes a **narcissistic wound**. This type of wound say's

> *"I have been badly hurt, to the core, and I need to protect myself at all costs.*

Now that we have defined what *betrayal trauma* is, and how it is quite different from the point of view that the betrayer holds, it is time to recognize what is happening in the moment for the one who was betrayed. Below is a description of some the most common symptoms.

How to Identify *Betrayal trauma* on Your Spouse

In the intensity of grief and loss of *Betrayal trauma*, Anger seems to come first, then disillusionment, leading to self-doubt and relational distancing. *Betrayal trauma* has identifiable stages and symptoms:

1. **Discovery, Anger, Shock, and Devastation.** The initial and subsequent discovery of your porn use by your spouse calls all your history and the marital history into question. Often with an insatiable need to extract painful confessions and many details, which in turn *embitters* the betrayed spouse, leading to a subconscious drive towards punishment. Grief follows with a feeling of being ungrounded, lost in chaos, emotional dysregulation, and ambiguous loss.

2. **Emotional Disruption.** Cognitive dissonance occurs when what we believe or want to be true does not align with what we see or know to be true. Signs of the progression of dissonance can be seen in how your spouse acts. When dissonance is active, it is often seen externally by unusual or strong reactions to circumstances that are markedly different than before the discovery. This may be over-reaction, under-reaction, standoffishness, or general crankiness. Often this is also seen as explosive and prolonged anger over simple matters.

3. **Physical signs.** Sleep deprivation, incessant worry, intrusive dreams, loss of appetite, nausea, headaches, and other symptoms of worry or anxiety.

4. **Emotional signs:** Negativity, low energy, highly exaggerated mood swings, criticism, gallows humor, and distancing.

5. **Behavioral signs.** In some cases, there is an obsession with making sure the two of you go to bed and stay in bed the whole time together. In her mind, this may keep you under control and lessen her stress. In addition, the following behaviors may become common:

- Watching you closely and a desire to know where you are and what you are doing at all times.
- Need or demand to look at your phone randomly.
- Examining your search history.
- Walking in on you randomly to "catch you" if possible.
- Testing your patience with criticism, impatience, or demands.
- Keeping you busy with lists of chores.
- Clinging on in an unusual manner.
- The need to be in control of the family as an organization, being in charge rather than partnering.

Your Reactions Trigger or Amplify Spouse's Traumatic Stress

Look at the list below. These are the five most common deflections that an addict will use when confronted by someone who knows the truth. Mark each of these that you have used when your wife is reacting to stress, and you are reacting to her.

☐ Blame-shifting

☐ Gaslighting (revising the truth to support the addict)

☐ Criticism and verbal attacks

☐ Expressing extreme anger.

☐ Withdrawing physically, psychologically, or physically from the relationship. (abandoning).

What are you hoping will happen when you use one or more of the five tactics when you are being called out by your wife?

What do you suppose these tactics do to her, how do they alter how she sees you, what is the long-term effect on the relationship?

Anger Triggers

Anger is the result of being upset by what we interpret as an event that is intolerable to us. That event triggers a feeling, like jealousy, abandonment, fear, etc. Anger is our defense against that feeling; an attempt to control or repair the event we find intolerable. Anger is not a core emotion—it is a response to some other feeling.

Knowing what triggers your anger is knowing what you are feeling below the anger and why. Below is a list of some more common feelings/beliefs which tend to trigger anger in people.

Think about occasions when you have become angry and place a check next to any/all that are *likely* to be your own anger sources.

Relationship	Self-Esteem	Justice
☐ Abandoned	☐ Belittled	☐ Cheated
☐ Disconnected	☐ Controlled	☐ Disrespected
☐ Rejected	☐ Inferior	☐ Invalidated
☐ Neglected	☐ Devalued	☐ Judged
☐ Unloved	☐ Worthless	☐ Accused
	☐ Failure	

Table 1: Anger Sources

Now, from the list above, place your top 5 in order of *most likely* to trigger anger, i.e. which are the biggest triggers.

1. _____
2. _____
3. _____
4. _____
5. _____

From your list of the top five sources of anger, think about how you can identify which events, words, actions, feelings, etc. commonly *activate* these triggers in your marriage or romantic partnership. Make a list of as many as come to mind.

1. _____
2. _____

3. _____

4. _____

5. _____

Keep going if you can…

Differences Across the Gender Divide

It is typically true that for most men and women, anger is triggered by identifiably predictable clusters of feelings based on gender. This is *partly* due to biology, but it is also *reinforced by* how we *experience* social rules while growing up.

o   If you are female, it is highly likely that you have identified that your top triggers come from feelings of disconnection (relationship cluster).

o   If you are a male, it is highly likely that you have identified that your top triggers come from feelings of being controlled (self-esteem cluster).

Now, look back at Table 1: *Anger Sources* and see which cluster seems to have the most checked off. This will tell you where anger is coming from, and where you *think* it would lead when resolution when activated.

— **Relationship**

— **Self-Esteem**

— **Justice**

Gender will not *force* you into one group or the other. However, most people grow up in what would be called **typical social settings** where the group *reinforces* expectations upon the individual, usually determined by gender. e.g. boys are socially punished for crying; girls are socially punished for going against the group.

Stages of Recovery for the Betrayed

In your recovery from porn or cybersexual addiction you are going to quickly discover that **your** progress will **not recover** your spouse from her own trauma caused by the discovery of your addiction. There are multiple stages that need to be completed, some for you, some for her, and some together. Since it all starts from trauma (hers is the discovery, yours is the revelation of your secret) the recoveries need to begin with each of you individually by addressing the traumatic content of your lives.

1. **Revelation.** For the betrayed spouse, discovery triggers traumatic shock and devastation along with emotional outrage: hurt, fear, anger, fury, bitterness, rage. Depression, doubt, and unknowing (ambiguity).

When Betrayal Happens...
Restoration takes a Process

Revealation	RECOVER	REPAIR	RESTORE	REFRIEND
The day of Discovery is traumatic for the betrayed spouse, and one of debilitating shame for the betraying spouse. Accepting and withstanding the crisis of infidelity and discovery takes special care • • •	For the Betraying Spouse, special education and coaching will allow you to break the habits that led to toxic choices, and recover a sense of Christian marriage with true leadership once more • • •	The weight of Betrayal Trauma goes beyond words. The betrayed spouse needs information and tools to establish safety in order to prepare for future restoration of trust in the marriage • • •	Making a marriage function once more after a betrayal must include a new level of Safety and Trust. Once the couple has learned to move beyond the hurt and trauma to a new understanding, it's time to begin to restore the process communication with a new goal of moving forward • • •	After discovering a betrayal, and in many cases long before the betrayal occurred, the FRIENDLINESS in your marriage was lost. Of the three needed components of marriage, friendship is perhaps the most emotionally crucial for long term success. The final step in recovering from betrayal is to find friendship once again • • •
Trauma	Change	Safety	Function	Transform

Recovering Your Covenant Marriage

2.   **Recovery.** This is in two separate parts: For the betraying spouse (addict), a healing of the self and recovery from the addiction. For the betrayed spouse, a recovery of self from the overwhelming doubt, fear, and ambiguity of grief. Since these two recoveries are independent, they will not happen at the same rate, but both must occur substantially before any serious repair can be made to the relationship.

3.   **Repair.** At this stage, it becomes possible to begin to repair the broken relationship directly. This is the beginning of healing and is still very painful as safety is reestablished and trust is tested.

4.   **Restoration.** The stage occurs when both you and your spouse begin to move forward in life once more. This may not be constant, but it is restoration in process. Functionality begins to return to the marriage, and the great divide is less pronounced. Restoration and redefining of the marital *Love Story* is now the focus of the relationship.

5. **Re-friending** comes when the two of you are once more reconciled and can enjoy each other once more despite the past. At this point, marriage ceases to be a constant renegotiation of hurts, and instead focuses on collaborative strategies to make a great outcome in life.

One obstacle to your spouse's recovery from the shock and devastation of your porn addiction occurs when belief or the instruction of others tells her that she must immediately forgive you. While choosing to forgive for the sake of Christian duty is laudable, the demand to do so before she is ready will amplify the hurt. This is like blaming the victim for their own pain.

Her own fear and distrust of you and the need to have safety does not just go away. It comes in the process we see as *grief*, just like if someone dies. It takes time to renegotiate life and meaning, and how she fits into the marriage post-discovery. Well-meaning friends and pastors often try to convince the betrayed spouse that their first responsibility is to forgive and support you in your quest to recover from your problem. Frankly, this is not her job, and is asking too much. Unrecognized or unsupported grief metastasizes into an emotional cancer that will tear her and the marriage apart. The first battle she must wage is navigating her new reality and becoming safe once more. Until she does this, she will remain stuck in grief even while you recover. Anger is a powerful symptom of grief.

The full range of recovery through Refriending looks like this:

- Traumatic shock and devastation.

- Emotional outrage: hurt, fear, anger, fury, bitterness, rage.

- Depression, doubt, and unknowing (ambiguity).

- Recovering and healing of the self.

- Recovery and healing of the Relationship

- Moving on...The stage when both you and your spouse begin to move forward in life once more. This may not be constant, but it is restoration in process.

- Re-friending comes when the two of you are once more despite the past.

This program is designed only to address *your recovery* by first helping you *see her recovery needs*, so that while you are doing your work, you will be able to help her, or at least not make it worse for her.

Betrayal Trauma and Your Relationship Status

Before we move on, I think it is important to understand that your spouse's state of healing about her *betrayal trauma* will have a tremendous impact on you and the marriage, even *if* you were to do everything correctly at this point. Since it is unlikely that you are doing everything correctly, it is critical that you consider some of the impacts that her state of mind has on the marriage, so that you do not defend your own self and your own efforts, and thereby risk causing her more harm. Remember that for her, your infidelity is still active until at some point she believes that true change is taking place in you. This will come much later than any changes you believe are visible in you.

The matrix below is a representation of the two primary axes that she will be struggling with, the relational safety axis, and the love vs contempt axis. Safety is about fear vs trust. Right now, her fear is likely at peak negativity. This is understandable. You have hurt her deeply and shocked her out of the safe space that the marriage is supposed to provide. So, she is fearful and unable to trust you yet. A lot of time is needed before you see much change in this axis. The second axis is the *way* she is seeing you. Love sees the good in people, excusing and allowing for a lot of mistakes. Contempt is the opposite of love. It sees the bad in people, and is unlikely to accept mistakes, and more likely will assign ill intentions as motive as an extension of your betrayal. When contempt is high, feelings and beliefs about her love for you will naturally be low.

The Matrix shows how these two axes combine to place the relationship at risk. With maximum contempt and maximum fear (distrust) the relationship will be volatile. You will fight more, she will experience hurt more easily, and she will be driven by instinct to punish you for hurting her. This is a natural human reaction to intimate hurts. The subconscious goal is to demonstrate to you how much she is hurting by hurting you. She isn't doing it to be vindictive, but to beg for your attendance to her hurt. But it will feel, look, and act like vindictiveness. Don't let that cause you to be defensive or argumentative. That will only fuel fear and contempt, delaying her recovery and amplifying the risk to the marriage's survival.

When love is still intact, but fear is high, the risk is more moderate, but still there. It can produce clinginess and neediness in your spouse. This is her way of trying to get proof that you are not a monster, and that you do love her, and that the relationship will be okay. But the risk is still significant, and much of your responsiveness or apathy to her needs will press her towards fear or contempt.

Betrayal Trauma Matrix

When love is low, but trust is still offered, there will likely be an atmosphere of criticism and aggression. This is a response to hold you responsible to act properly and confirm her trust level. It will NOT feel very much like trust to you, and you are at risk of reacting as if you are being controlled and punished. If you react to this feeling, you will activate her distrust, and will quickly see your relationship decay back to high-risk territory.

Obviously, the goal is for the love levels to increase along with the trust levels. When this begins to stabilize, openness and a more welcoming presence returns to the marriage. This does don't mean that you are out of the woods, but it will take your marriage out of the daily risk of failure.

All the success or failure in navigating the matrix is *driven* by *her perception* of the two factors but is *decided* by your *chosen reactions* to her automatic responses and coping strategies. When she is fearful, and you try to tell her she can trust you, her fear will increase because insecurity is already high, and she will see you as manipulating, gaslighting, or outright lying, even if you are sincere. When she feels contemptuous in the moment, and you defend yourself against unfair or inaccurate judgements or rejection, she will see this as narcissistic.

Your reaction must always be validating of her current feeling state. You do not have to agree with her conclusions, but you must not argue the validity of her feelings.

"I understand you are angry and feel that I am not to be trusted. If I were in your situation, because of the hurt I caused you, I would feel and believe the same way. I am so sorry that I have placed you in this position, and I am trying to do everything I can to keep you safe now and in the future. But I know that you can't see that now, and I understand."

Victim Empathy

The Victim Impact Statement

"Why am I being asked to do this Exercise?" Pornography abuse or addiction does not happen in a vacuum. For men who are married, in a relationship, or who have children, there are always victims of your choices. Even if you are single, there are victims. Once you begin to explore how your choices violate another person or people, you unlock some of the most powerful motivators for change.

This example is to help you begin the process of identifying victims of your behavioral choices. Once you have a list of victims, you will be asked to complete a Victim Impact Statements (VIS). These statements will help you to walk in the shoes of the people you are impacting when you make the choice to use pornography.

For each VIS, describe in the first person, as if you are that person, all the thoughts, feelings, and outcomes that have or may exist. The VIS is to be constructed as if your victim wrote a letter to the court or victim advocate for the purpose of healing, or speaking up for self, even as a prosecutor's tool to help determine appropriate punishment. Don't confuse this with the 12-step process of making amends. This is not about you, it's about her, her feelings, and what she has experienced.

How to Write a Good Impact Statement

Good impact statements are informative and reliable. Impact statements differ in the nature of the victimization, the relationship to the person who caused the victim to suffer, and the necessary details, which makes it difficult to provide a specific format or template. Regardless of what kind of impact statement you are planning to write, the examples below should provide insight and guidance. However, you might find this task easier with some tips to guide you:

- Gather relevant information and facts you need.

- Determine grouping of the content. An outline would be helpful.

- Start out broad using details and imagery to make the victim's voice heard, then narrow to the central focus (consequences of the victimization), then summarize with a decisive action statement.

- Proofread for clarity and logic.

The samples below are suggestions, not necessarily required formats...

Sample Emotional Abuse VIS

I realize things are better, but they are always good for a while, and they are only good because I stay quiet. As long as I am quiet, you are happy. But I am not.

I stay quiet because you shut me down as well as your inability to be civil or accept any correction, criticism, or consequence. I have made several attempts only to have you dismiss me or put me through the ringer and berate me, deflect, and project before you finally apologize for your reaction. By that time, you have committed so many other offenses that the original issue is lost in the conflict and pales in comparison.

Resentment is the bottom line. Since our last blowout, there have many offenses, and I am left to deal with all of it alone or with my counselor. In the meantime, you continue along the same path, feeling entitled to my loyalty, expecting me to cater to jealousies and insecurities I did not create, blissful in denial, sweeping everything under the rug and happy to ignore reality.

I do not care to talk to you about it anymore. I do not care to list it all for you. I do not need you to validate how I feel or acknowledge all that has happened in order for me to know it is all true. Just know that the most offensive of all is that I have been in therapy for 10 months, in between beatings and verbal assaults, as a result of said beatings and verbal assaults, while you continue along the same path. You know all this, but you push it out of your mind completely. It is more important for you to maintain your own comfort at the expense of mine, even though I have none. This is not love.

You will never see this letter because you are not entitled to it. I do not owe you the respect of notice or warning, since you never gave me any for the 3 years you maligned, slandered, and assaulted me. Funny enough, as angry as I am with myself more than with you, I do not wish you any ill. I truly hope that you will find the happiness that awaits a sober and anger-free human being.

Sample of Adultery VIS

When we met, I thought I was the luckiest person alive. You made me feel special, and I offered you my heart, and my faith, and my trust. But you wanted much more. You deceived me. You lied to me. You cheated on me. Over the years, as I continued to trust and honor you, you debased our vows by choosing to pollute the soul of our relationship with others. Now, I am destroyed. I do not know if I can ever get over the pain, because it has stained my entire outlook. I cannot allow myself to trust you, and now, I wonder if I can ever truly trust others. What my parents took such care to install in me, my faith in the basic goodness of family and loved ones, the ability to trust that life could be happy with those loved ones around me, has now been damaged.

You were supposed to be my safe place. That one person who put me above all others. That one person who I could share the most intimate and vulnerable parts of me that I dare not let anyone else see or feel. You were the one who I was supposed to be able to rely on when I needed assurance. When life got hard, or people hurt me, you were the one who I chose to believe would be my safety net. You robbed me of that most sacred space. You invited others into our shared life without my permission, without my knowledge. I am no longer safe with you, because I will never truly know again that I am the most important person to you.

Now it is time to make a list of all those people who your addictive behavior has victimized:

_____

_____

_____

_____

_____

_____

_____

Using the list above, write a victim impact statement for each of these people, starting with the one who had reason to trust you the most. Take your time and imagine what it would be like if you were that person. Then, speak out in the first person as if you were that person.

As you finish each VIS, print it out and give it to your counselor, or bring it to the group to read to the group.

Making Her Safe Again

Rebuilding Safety

The first step to recovering from betrayal is to recover safety. Mistrust, anger, fear, and many related emotions come from the sudden loss of safety. The rebuilding of safety in marriage is a two-person mission. As the betraying spouse, it is primarily your responsibility to change the variables that make your wife unsafe. it is her responsibility to set boundaries to prevent you from transgressing her safety going forward. This only works when both of you understand the need and engage in a conversation that produces a NEW WAY of protecting the marriage and her from what you had before. Safety is not a return to life prior to the discovery of betrayal, because something in that life allowed the betrayal to occur. The goal is to establish a new way of living life as a couple post-betrayal. It begins with you, the betraying spouse, learning to understand what happened to her when you violated your covenant.

Our goal when reestablishing relationship post-betrayal is to work first to secure the bond and attachment between both of you once again. For your part, you need to see what you did and did not do that left her attachment damaged. Then you can take steps to stop the problem (step one of healing) and proceed to repair the empathic wounds (step two of healing), finally to begin the final stage of rebuilding the marital relationship. It all starts with understanding safety by hearing what she has lost.

When a wife has been hurt by intimate betrayal, whether that is adultery, porn addiction, lying, emotional affairs, or other forms of infidelity to your vows, her feeling of SAFETY inside the marriage is damaged, often destroyed. It is your responsibility to keep her safe, so it is now your responsibility to repair what you broke.

Listening and Understanding

To help your wife find safety again, you need to apply deep empathy to your relationship. Empathy is most simply defined as "the ability to understand and share the feelings of another."

Deep empathy is nothing more than going deeper in your attempt to know and relate with her as closely as possible. You can only do this by listening intensely to her descriptions of her feelings, thoughts, and experiences. To listen, you do not offer instruction, opinions, or fixes. You listen…carefully…and try to memorize exactly what she is saying. Particularly attend to the feeling words or the feeling-based meaning of what she is sharing.

Example:

> *"I am so tired of hearing you say you are sorry but then you keep doing the same thing. I feel like you do not really care about me. It is like you forget what you did to me and then do it again. That is why I do not trust you."*

What is she saying?

- *so tired* = She is worn out hoping and anticipating then being disappointed.

- *you keep doing* = you are not being sincere about your apologies because you do not follow through.
- *feel like* = My feelings are telling me that what I want to believe is not what is happening and that causes me to fear.
- *do not really care* = I am not important to you.
- *you forget* = I am not a priority to you in life.
- *did to me* = You hurt me, and I am suffering, and you do not recognize this completely.
- *do it again* = You are still hurting me despite all you say and all I express to you about how much it hurts.
- *do not trust you* = until you stop hurting me, show that you understand me, and show me that you are making REAL changes, I am stuck in fear and do not feel safe in our marriage, in my life, and in my mind.

How might you restate her meaning using the above level of understanding to let her know you have truly heard her? The answer is to *repeat what she is meaning and feeling* to the best of your ability. Use *her words*, when possible, use *her meaning* as best as you understand it if feeling words were not given to you.

Example:

> *"You are feeling unsafe and scared because you have no way of knowing that I really understand the pain I've caused you."* (This is only a partial statement of the above facts.)

Exercise:

Using the bulleted items above, write out a full restatement of what this spouse is trying to communicate, like the example above, but use all the content. Try to say it with the voice of the injured spouse, not your projection of what you would want her to say.

Dimensions of Safety in Marriage

Sexual Safety. Men routinely fail to recognize the level of trust and risk that women must experience when being sexually intimate with a man. This has as much to do with the actual act of sex as it does with the relational aspects. For a woman to invite sexual action, she gives up some control over her body. Simultaneously, she must trust the man is sincere in his care and respect for her as a person in relationship, not as an object of pure lust.

Many men do not see sexual intimacy as a deep relational test, but more like an activity of pleasure and hopefully, as an expression of passion. But relational intimacy is not just sex to most women. To be sexually safe, women must feel and believe that they are engaged at the heart and mind, not just the body. Trust and safety are needed to safeguard her heart and soul.

Emotional Safety. Emotional safety is also indelibly connected to relational safety for most women. Emotional-relational safety means that she can trust and rely on her feelings about you, about herself, and about the two of you. Relationships are like self-esteem. Relationships tell us we are okay. When emotionally challenged, it is normal for women to reevaluate the state of the relationship. This means reevaluating multiple parts of the relationship, from who they are to you, to how they know who you truly are, to whether or not they somehow missed seeing important evidence about you, herself, and your relationship as a whole. Emotional safety requires thoughts to align with facts and feelings so that your spouse can trust her emotional response to events.

Physical Safety. Physical safety can mean exactly that, if physical harm has occurred, or if she has a history of family violence or former relationships where she was in harm's way. But physical safety also means her home stability. E.g., are you reliably employed, are you emotionally explosive, are you causing her to stay on alert around you? Do you or she feel the need to leave and stay elsewhere when things are difficult? Is there talk of divorce? Do the children get agitated when they see or hear the two of you argue...? Stability and physical safety go together. Knowing you are okay, and that you have family, shelter, food, love, etc. are all essential to a sense of physical health and wellbeing.

Spiritual Safety. Faith-based couples naturally consider spiritual aspects of their safety in relationship. Yet all human beings are spiritual beings, even when they are not religious, or faith based. Spirituality includes faith, but also self-identity and philosophical views of life. Existential well-being might be said to contain a sense of who you are and how you and others relate to one another. For the faith-based couple, this starts with an identity in God, then and identity of self, then an identity in marriage, family, and so forth. When spiritually unsafe, what is compromised is self-identity. Self-identity for a believer is accepting and knowing self through the eyes of God. But we also seek confirmation on self from the reflection of others. When someone treats us badly, then allows us to feel we are somehow less than okay in our identity, we forget what God says and take this as evidence that we are not okay.

Women are particularly vulnerable to believing that they are not good enough or attractive enough when betrayed by an intimate person like a spouse, parent, or close friend. They doubt their worth. This brings spiritually unsafe status to the forefront, self-doubt, and vulnerability to shaming. When a husband betrays a wife, she also begins to doubt his spiritual stability, and is threatened in her own choice to follow or submit when she no longer has faith in his sincerity of faith. It creates a negative cycle of doubt.

Finally, making your spouse spiritually safe includes taking up true leadership once again, or perhaps even for the first time. Christian marriage is founded on God's command for the governance of the marriage and society, which places a responsibility and burden on the husband to lead. When women are unsafe, it forces them to take the lead out of fear that the husband is unable or unworthy. To restore faith and dispel fear, he must learn to lead in a safe and biblically sound way.

Stop Making Her Unsafe!

Now that you understand how to listen better, and how to respond in a helpful way, your task becomes a direct effort to make her safe once again in all four dimensions: Sexually, Emotionally, Physically, and Spiritually. This begins by first halting any behavior that makes her UN-safe. Only after you stop making her unsafe can you take steps to help restore lost safety.

Example:

Using these four dimensions of safety, take a fearless look at your behavior (attitudes, words, actions, etc.) and see what is happening that threatens your wife's safety in each dimension.

Make a list of the top 3-5 things you are doing or not doing that activate her into feeling or thinking she is no longer safe.

Now, considering the list you made above, what can you do to change or stop what you have been doing and thereby stop activating her unsafe feelings? *List them out in writing....*

Making Safety Your Mission

Now that you have identified what you have done, and must stop doing, it is time to consider what you can begin doing that will help restore her safety.

Marriage should be the ultimate safe space between two people. Just like taking refuge in the safety of God for the individual.

> *Keep me safe, O God, for in you I take refuge (Psalm 16:1).*

Marriage is a refuge for the couple.

> *"...husbands should love their wives as their own bodies. He who loves his wife loves himself. For no one ever hated his own flesh, but nourishes and cherishes it, just as Christ does the church (Ephesians 5:28-29).*

Our relationship with God and with a spouse is based on a level of intimacy made possible when it is first safe enough to be vulnerable. With God, this means to trust His word about who He is and what He sees in you. With a spouse, it is the same. Trusting that a spouse is who he or she says they are is essential to a marriage vision, and believing in who that spouse sees you as is equally critical. When a betrayal occurs, these two foundational elements are damaged or lost, at least for a while. It takes major effort to restore marital trust effectively.

Exercise:

Using the same three to five items you identified in part two that threatened your spouse's safety, look at yourself and how you can proactively prevent future threats to her safety. In other words, how can you change yourself for the long-term?

Exercise:

For the last step, look at the list of safety dimensions once again. Identify ways you can enhance and protect her safety going forward in your marriage. Think of this plan as the perfect expression of her safety and make it a series of statements that operationalize your actions for the rest of your marriage.

Write them out.

- Sexual Safety for My Wife...
- Emotional Safety for My Wife...
- Physical Safety for My Wife...
- Spiritual Safety for My Wife...

Finally, take all of this written work and have a deep conversation with your wife.

- Share this material with her, let her know what you have discovered so far.
- Ask her if what you have concluded is correct or not.
- Then, ask her what you missed or failed to notice.
- Then, once you are sure that you have understood her safety needs, make a vow to her to begin today to act accordingly, to prove your deeper understanding.

This level of vulnerability from you is the only way to truly begin to resolve the safety issue in your marriage.

I suggest you make some notes from your conversation so you can keep things in mind going forward.

Communication = Relationship

Communication is a Skill.

There is no peace without holding a common interest. Amos 3:3 asks whether two can walk together unless they are in agreement? The answer is no. Not if they are doing it *together*. Commonality comes through understanding. Understanding comes from effective communication. Communication is synonymous with relationship. Relationships exist within some level of agreement. Until there is communication (congress) between people, relationships are not possible. The words are synonymous.

Communication comes in many different forms. You have heard that 90-95% of communication is non-verbal, leaving only 5-10% for actual words. While this number has many critics, research does support that non-verbal communication makes up at least 70% or more of communication. This means both the sending of information, and the receiving and interpretation of contextual meaning.

Interpretation tends to be faulty because of noise. Noise in the communication channel takes on many faces. Tonal quality, infliction, physical gestures, posture, eye contact. All of these things plus many micro expressions leak into the communication channel and alter meaning and interpretations. Inconsistencies between spoken words and nonverbal behavior alter meaning.

When you are at the negotiating table, pay attention to how your counterparts speak and act. Do the words they are saying match the way they are carrying themselves? Look at the people who are not talking—what does their body language signal to you? Remember that their spoken words only account for about seven percent of their communication and look for nonverbal cues that contradict their words. It is also important that you make sure your own nonverbal messages are in line with what you are saying. If your facial expressions are pained, or you cannot maintain eye contact, you are communicating insecurity to your counterpart no matter what you say.

The 93% of communication is nonverbal comes from Albert Mehrabian's 7-38-55 rule. He wrote that it is the impact of nonverbal communication, communication that is observed, which directly impacts interpretation of meaning. This theory has been with us since the early seventies. It is commonly held by those who teach and apply communication theory, particularly those who work directly in relationship-oriented fields such as counseling. Mehrabian's theory focuses on the impact of nonverbal messaging for the interpretation of meaning. Nonverbal communication includes all communication that is not spoken with words and includes many facets of communication. Of particular note in Mehrabian's theory are tone of voice and body language.

Using the 7-38-55 rule:

Participating in a conversation face to face allows you to derive meaning from the conversation. However, you are likely to assign meaning based on more than the actual context of the words. So, before you can focus on a true win-win, you need to understand the elements of the 7-38-55 rule, and the biases that come with them.

The likelihood of misinterpretation during the course of communicating is actually extremely high. Even with keen observation, most people misconstrue the actual meaning intended by others routinely. Listening to the words without observing nonverbals will result in misinterpretation when communication is personal. This is why we see so many conflicts erupt when couples use text messaging to communicate important information in our contemporary culture. A text message is using words, which is a mere 7% of the *content* in normal communication. The remaining 93% must be inferred by the recipient, perhaps with minimal help from an emoji. When the receiver is already anticipating a negative response, they will most likely infer the most negative intents.

To help illustrate how communication functions, and to drive home the point that your communication skills and mindfulness in a conversation weighs heavily in conflicts, we will begin by looking at the distinct parts of communication. Then, we will examine a simple tool that, when used, will help you to overcome the natural biases and errors that assign meaning rather than accurately understanding meaning:

Words are important. Despite the ever-present impact of the nonverbals, the *actual words* are the *intention* of the effort to communicate. The 7-38-55 rule estimates that only 7% of communication comes from words. This may or may not be accurate, but it is indicative of the tendency in people to drift from intended content, often because of stress or interpretation errors (assumptions). The words we use can drift when bringing up examples or defensive statements, and other noise to the communication channel. Picking words and hearing accurately assure both sides of the channel to say and hear. However, there is other noise that tends to disrupt. Vocal tone outweighs actual words by about 500%!

Tone is powerful. According to the 7-38-55 rule vocal tone accounts for 38% of the conveyed or perceived meaning. This is a dual process. The sender can telegraph contempt, anger, frustration, and a plethora of other emotions with a slight alteration of tone. Likewise, the receiver can decode words based on how they interpret tone and reassign meaning. Tone is hard to disguise, and it is hard to overlook. To assure correct communication of meaning, tone must be managed, and understanding (assumptions) should be verified using precision of words. Asking for clarity is the first defense against the noise of tone. Remember, tone may intend a meaning, or it may be misperceived. Assuming everyone reads tone the same is a major assumption, and most often leads to confusion or hurt.

Body language. This last 55% is huge in its impact, bigger than tone and words combined. Body language is automatic most of the time. It is learned and mimicked. It is practiced and perfected. It sends meaning subliminally or explicitly. Eye rolls, neck rolls, pointing a finger, shushing gestures, raised fists, crossed arms, gasps, sighs… All of these are things we see, use, and quickly interpret. Sometimes the meaning is clear. Other times it is not. Again, precision of language is needed to verify meaning before an informed interpretation should be settled on.

Nonverbals are immensely powerful. Observing other's nonverbals is essential to understanding. But just as important are your own nonverbals when listening and responding. One way you can immediately improve your own communication is by calibrating your own nonverbals intentionally, by focusing on how the other person in your communication feels, reacts, or responds.

When I was a counseling student, my skills professor began by teaching us an acronym, SOLER. This stood for Square, Open, Lean in, Eye contact, and Relaxed. These defined an effective counseling posture that would enhance both the client's perception of our attention to their words (body language), and to focus our attention on the client (mindful attending). In talking to your spouse, do you find in retrospect that you fail to sit facing her Squarely, or fail to maintain Open body language? Perhaps you cross your arms or turn to one side? Do you show intense attention by Leaning in towards the conversation, or do you lean back and add distance? How about Eye contact? Do you meet her eyes appropriately while she is speaking, or do you stare into space, at your phone, or watch TV? Are you Relaxed as you listen, or are you tense, braced for an assault or poised to escape? All of these elements activate volumes of communicated messages that your wife will be reading automatically. Consider how things could change if you applied SOLER when she is telling you something meaningful to her.

Empathy. Gaining a functional understanding for others, known as *empathy*. Using your natural empathetic ability while hearing and responding helps you to communicate responsively, rather than reactively. Empathy is not hard. It should come naturally. Your life's experiences, combined with your knowledge of your spouse or other close people should help you to understand their needs and point of view.

However, empathy is often distorted when the feelings in you are filtered through your own experiences in life, expectations, or the patterns that have been established between you and someone you are close to. People who know each other well tend to argue much more frequently and intensely than strangers and casual acquaintances. This is because we hold a *high context relationship* with them. The more you know of someone, the more experience you have dealing with someone, and the more practice you have in relating with someone, the more context exists between the two of you. In a utopian sense, this context should bring deeper love and understanding. You will know how to complete each other's sentences, sense when they are emotionally compromised or wounded, as well as when they are joyful or playful. Unfortunately, this contextual relationship is also full of negative memories, patterns of misbehavior, mistrust, or competition. This can drive you to make a lot of negative assumptions just as instantly as making empathetic ones.

When you receive information that *affects* you, your perception of the information causes an internal reaction.

The internal reaction sparks emotional responses, which are often nonverbally telegraphed to others. Since many feelings and beliefs trigger automatic reactions, facial expressions and other non-verbals can also be automatic. For instance, when you smell something unpleasant, you may wrinkle your nose, shake your head, put your hand to your face, or grimace. Your inner reaction leaks out through nonverbal communication as micro expressions.

Calibrating your nonverbals is less about consciously adjusting what you are projecting, and more about arriving at an accurate understanding of the content being sent to you. When you comprehend another's perspective accurately, your emotional and physical expression reflect the message being sent, not your personal interpretation of what you think you received. The actual position of a disagreement may not necessarily change, meaning you do not have agree with the message being sent to you. But your interpretation will be clearer.

Your goal is only to understand the other person's point of view and feelings *accurately*. If you hear accurately, and empathize selflessly, your nonverbal response will automatically telegraph empathic awareness. This skill, once developed, can be highly effective in resolving or preventing conflicts. Empathetic attending leaves the win/lose dilemma behind and seeks to relate.

Two Levels of Communication Your Wife Needs

First, you must develop your *listening skills*. Second, you must become *aware of your own purpose* behind your attempts to communicate. I have found that, when working with men, the first step can be developed best when taking the passive role in communicating at first. Over time, you can do both stages simultaneously, but the listening side of communication skills application is the more difficult to master, at least for men. Before we dive into this skill, I want to describe the *awareness matrix* so that you can see where you are headed and can also understand where your spouse is coming from.

Empathic attending is the process of listening with *intention to understand the feelings and needs* being communicated by someone else. It uses the mechanism of empathy to bring understanding. Most of us know that empathy is something we use to get into the perspective of another person, by applying our own feelings and experiences, so that we can vicariously experience the feelings of another person.

In empathic attending you must become aware of the other, suspend your own agenda, and reflect back what is being said to you as accurately as possible. If you miss the point, ignore the other's efforts at relating, attempt to solve their problem too swiftly, or shift the focus off their efforts, you will empathically fail. *Empathic failures* happen all the time. But when it happens in a significate moment an empathic wound can be inflicted. In the case of a betrayed or wounded marriage, there are already substantial wounds. Any new empathic wounds will compound or aggregate into a larger wound.

To be fair, you do not necessarily have to be wrong or do wrong for an empathic failure to occur. Many times, empathic failures are unavoidable. This is something we often discuss in group as men habitually step on a landmine unknowingly. For the wounded spouse, little awareness of your actual innocence or guilt for new wounds will matter. The fact that they are feeling wounded is enough to warrant your efforts to attend with the highest priority. Ben Shapiro is known for his saying, "facts don't care about your feelings." This is true. But in a wounded relationship you will also find that *feelings do not care about your facts*, and when you try to prove the facts, things just get worse. To understand how this happens, let us take a look at the awareness cycle in communication.

Awareness in Communication

When someone is trying to relate something important to you about their state of mind, feelings, fears, or needs, they do so on three levels.

1. **The first level tells you *where the issue is coming from*.** There are three sources from which need-based communication originate:

   Sensory Data: Sensory data would be found in a measurable or observable account of an event.

   - Description of an Event
   - Using real Facts
   - Relying on Personal Observations
   - Providing Examples
   - Reciting Figures

   Thoughts are usually beliefs or assumptions that are more or less decided upon by the individual and may not accurately reflect actual events.

   - Beliefs
   - Expectations
   - Opinions
   - Assumptions
   - Interpretations
   - Evaluations

   Feelings are the most difficult of the origin options since feelings are often based on fear, reactions, and phenomenological past events to which you are not privy. Remember, feelings do not care about facts!

- Emotions
- Fears
- Hurts
- Hope
- Body Sensations

Once you have identified the origin of any attempt at communication, if you are able to stay calm and purposeful, you can more accurately and expertly navigate and negotiate for the best outcome. More about that in the listing skills method below.

2. **The next level of awareness tells you w***ho is the issue focused on.*** This is not always obvious because much of the time, heated or feelings-based arguments spend a lot of time focusing on whoever is being targeted in the moment, and are not necessarily revealing the true focus. So, to understand the true subject of a focus, we start with wants.

First, who is the person that want is focused on?

- For Self (the speaker)
- For Relationship (the speaker plus another)
- For Others (this can be anyone in the speaker's circle of concern)

Next, we determine *what the speaker wants* for the person(s) they are trying to advocate for. To do this we try to understand the:

- Aspirations
- Intentions
- Dreams, hopes, and goals
- Longings

- Objectives

This list can help you, as a listener, hear more accurately what the speaker is telling you. For instance, your spouse is telling you about her mother.

> *"Mom was telling me her neighbor has a new boyfriend and they go out all the time. Mom says that her friend is so busy that it is hard to see how she is going to keep up with all of her other social obligations."* To illustrate her point, she relates her mom's recent complaint, *"She even told me how her friend was supposed to help her with a church decoration project but keeps cancelling there planning meetings because her boyfriend needs her to do something. Mom says she is getting all the work dumped on her."*

What is happening here? Using the awareness matrix, we can first determine where this focus is coming from. We can assume that there is some *data*, since your wife's mom is stating what looks to be *facts*. But there are also *feelings* here. The mom is frustrated, angry. Even jealous and feeling abandoned. So, the focus is dually driven, by facts that are triggering a belief of "unfair," which produces a *need* to share feelings. We would conclude that by the time it was told to your wife, it is a *feelings-based* issue.

Next, who is this issue focused on. It sounds like it would be the friend. But that would be unlikely. In this case, mom is focused on herself, and your wife is *focused on mom*. So, in the immediate conversation you are having with your spouse, you would say that your wife is focused on mom, specifically on mom's longings and objectives. She empathizes with mom's feelings of abandonment and loneliness, and therefore *wants you to hear that too*, and empathize with her as she empathizes with mom.

3. **Finally, we come to action,** *"What action Is being sought?"* There are many variables here. So, to help sort it out, we start with "is this a past, present, or future action?

Past action goals are about rehashing something that happened in the past. But, for the speaker, resolution was not achieved and so they are still trying to right the wrong.

Present action goals tend to focus more on stopping something that is active or seeking acknowledgment and repentance for something recent or active.

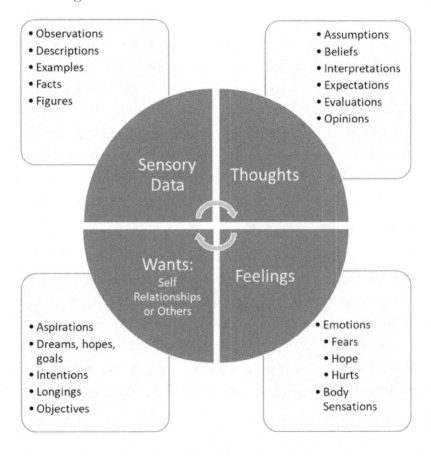

Future action goals are more about changes in future behavior, a return to a preferred outcome, clarification of direction, repentance and recovery, and other hopes for the future.

As you listen to your wife (or anyone who is trying to communicate from a place of emotional need), you will see the flow of awareness shift in you, as you attend empathically to their presentation. Just keep in mind, the speaker is not thinking about these awareness factors, so keep them to yourself. When you get your turn to share, you can construct questions to help you *verify your suspicions*, and hopefully bring awareness to the speaker as well.

Active Listening

Now that you have some idea what is driving the speaker to seek empathic connection with you, it is time to learn about your role, the role of the listener. In communication, there is a sender and a receiver. You can only be one of these effectively at any given time. I am sure you have experienced electronic feedback when a microphone is picking up the sounds from a speaker and the re-looping of the sound quickly becomes a shrill noise. In human-to-human communication, we have the same issue. Our feedback noise comes from having two outputs colliding with two inputs, where both are striving for dominance. Nothing but noise. In the real world we call this an argument.

When clients ask, I define levels of conflicted conversation as discussion, debate, argument, and fight. A **discussion** is a casual sharing of information that may or may not offer differences of opinion. They share insights or perhaps to deepen understanding between two people. A **debate** is where you are trying to persuade someone to your point of view with new or contradictory facts and information. Neither of these two conflicts are negative or toxic and can actually be healthy and necessary for intimate growth.

Arguments are riskier. This is where debate tends to get a bit more heated. There is a strong need on both sides to defend a previously held opinion, and a goal of proving or persuading only one point of view. Arguments are framed as win-lose scenarios. There is a drive to win, which means a desire to make the other person lose.

Fights happen when this win-lose becomes an imperative, and the parties forget about the risk to their relationship and go for the kill. Anger, shouting, breaking things, rage-quitting, threats, insults, and the like are all signs of fighting. To be fair, some fights are going to happen between all couples over time. But they should be so rare that you can count and name them easily, even over the course of years, because they were so unique. A good goal in a marriage is to know that if a fight should happen, it is a once in a year, or once in a decade event. If it is monthly, weekly, or daily, your marriage is toxic and needs help.

To prevent fights, listening skills are necessary to learn how to communicate actively and effectively. It starts with knowing that there are rules that you will both agree to follow. The most important rule is to listen to your partner until you fully understand what she wants you to know, *without adding your interpretation or perspective*. Or as Steven Covey puts it, "seek first to understand, then to be understood."[9]

Most of the time in a conflict, the sender is trying to convey something specific, while the receiver is only half listening. The receiver is actually having a second conversation in their own head, testing counterpoints, and planning a rebuttal. You know you do this. And, when you do, that silent conversation you have with yourself is one you always win. It is only when you present your point of view that things go wrong. The reason? Because you are *splitting* your attention between what the sender is sending and what you want to say. We call this split tasking, where you split your mental energy between two or more actions. The one that you judge most important will get about eighty percent of your attention, and the other task, listening in this case, gets twenty percent or less.

Human beings are lousy listeners. We want our turn at bat, to validate our beliefs, defend our actions, or otherwise maintain our self-image. But if you want a healthy relationship, you MUST have healthy communication. Remember, *communication* and *relationship* are synonymous. They define each other. Healthy communication brings healthy relationships. Unhealthy relationships drive unhealthy communication. The quickest way to heal a relationship is to stop talking and to start listening *intentionally* to whatever it is your partner wants you to hear.

The diagram below demonstrates a simple but highly effective method(tool) to hear and comprehend completely. Do this and you will find immediate improvement in your relationship. Do this and you will find a dramatic decrease in conflicts that usually build into arguments or fights. Do this and you will find an increase in true intimacy between you and your spouse.

Many men have told me this seems too complicated to do actively. I call that *resistance*. People tend to resist change, and this technique takes effort, and at first seems to deny a fair and balanced conversation, perhaps even forcing the husband into a corner to admit wrongdoing. But I promise you, it is much simpler in action than it looks on paper. And, when done correctly, you will have a better chance of having your side heard too or find that your side is actually not very different from hers to begin with. The steps are simple and may or may not repeat during one listening session.

The Listening Cycle

1. Attend. Attending happens when you actively use your curiosity to understand your spouse. Making good eye contact,

not talking, not thinking about your rebuttal, and being present with her is what attending requires. Look, listen, track, feel with her. Focus on her. Keep all distractions out of the picture, even when you hear a flaw in her argument. Let it go and listen to her intended meaning and feelings. This is the first thing that counselors learn to do. Attend, be present, do not judge, seek to understand.

2. Acknowledge. Acknowledging means repeating (as closely to her actual words as possible) what she has just told you. You are a mirror, and your job is to reflect what she is saying. This does two major things that affect your understanding. First, it clarifies whether or not you heard correctly. Second, it tells her you are indeed listening. To acknowledge, simply repeat, reflect, or report back what you just heard. A trick you can use to help you is to listen intentionally for any feeling words she uses, like frustrated, angry, sad, lonely, and repeat them back to her. If she did not use any feeling words, you can sometimes infer her feelings from the meaning of her words and offer a check-in of your understanding. E.g., "It sounds like this has really frustrated you." By using feeling language, you will connect heart-to-heart instead of head-to-head.

3. Ask for more. For this step, we are assuming you have already acknowledged her words, and she confirmed or corrected your understanding. Now is the time to invite more information. Ask her for details that would help you hear better or check in on what you think is going on. Use an open question, (questions that can't be answered with yes or no), or other tools to invite deeper understanding. Resist at all costs the temptation to add or tell her what you are thinking, or what she might have missed. Do not add any new information to her story. It is for her to tell, even if you think she's missing something or is dead wrong in her belief. *Never* jump in at this point and assume you were right so far, believing that it is safe to tell her your solution or perspective. You just want to see if there is anything that is left out from *her* point of view.

Once you have invited and been answered, you should **repeat step two** and *check your understanding* with a paraphrase of understanding. If the situation is complicated, you may need to repeat steps 2 and 3 multiple times. Only when your spouse tells you or agrees that you are hearing correctly are you safe to move on to step four.

4. Summarize and Take Responsibility. I have grouped these two components together because you need to act on them simultaneously. The summary follows effective closure of steps 2 and 3 and will include taking responsibility. Here is where most men get tripped up. Burn this into your memory now: taking responsibility for how she feels about something you have done is *different* from you being at fault. Many men fail here because they are thinking behind the scenes that they have their own facts that have not been presented which will exonerate or defend their actions. If you fall into this trap, you will undo all the effort you have just made.

Taking responsibility only *acknowledges* that, from your wife's unique point of view, that you are at fault and are the reason she is upset right now. You are *accepting* her perspective on the matter and working to help her heal. For example, if she thought you were not taking your counseling homework seriously because she did not see the effort you were putting in while working on it alone, she may get scared that you are going to relapse. That fear makes her act more edgy and aggressive. She may say, *"I do not think you're taking things seriously enough. I am worried you are going back to porn."* But you know that you are doing your homework, you are not doing porn, and you feel you are beating this addiction. Nevertheless, now is not the time to focus on *you.* Focus instead on her fear. *"Honey, I hear your fear and understand how hard this is for you because I have hurt you and you are afraid that I will do it again. I do not ever want that to happen again. I am sorry I brought you to this place and truly regret failing you."*

This is hard because male pride hates being told it is less than the champion. The unspoken priority of men is to maintain their image of acceptability to the world, without which men fear rejection and insignificance. So, in the event you are being unfairly judged, you will reactively and reflexively. want to defend yourself. Do not do this, not with your spouse! It may not be accurate, but as far as your spouse is concerned, it is real because it feels real to her in the moment. If you defend yourself at this point, you will only confirm her fears. So, by taking responsibility for how she feels (because you did bring her here) you will begin to assuage those fears.

5. Make Repairs. An empathic repair is simple, provided that you first resist the urge to correct her, or for your own point of view to be seen as right. By acknowledging and taking responsibility for how your wife *perceives* the relationship through the filter of your faulty actions, you set up an empathic understanding of her needs and her point of view. Repairing the wound is an attempt to bring healing by restoring what was lost. In her words, if you listened, you heard what she wanted. If she is scared, she wants assurances.

If she is angry, she needs you to acknowledge your actions. Using the awareness process matrix, you can see what actions are desired, and then do your best to follow through, first with your words, then with true action. Study the matrix until it makes sense to you.

Recalling the awareness cycle we just used to understand where your wife's perspective comes from, apply the same to your own desire or drive to be seen as correct. Remember, what you might see as facts and data, may be connected to past events that cause strong beliefs and feelings. These can cloud your judgment just as much as it clouds hers.

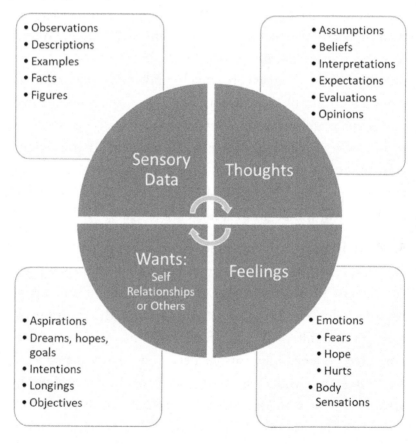

- Observations
- Descriptions
- Examples
- Facts
- Figures

- Assumptions
- Beliefs
- Interpretations
- Expectations
- Evaluations
- Opinions

Sensory Data

Thoughts

Wants:
Self
Relationships
or Others

Feelings

- Aspirations
- Dreams, hopes, goals
- Intentions
- Longings
- Objectives

- Emotions
- Fears
- Hope
- Hurts
- Body Sensations

Rediscovering the Self

Who is Driving Your Emotional Vehicle?

When an adult has a history of childhood trauma, adverse childhood experiences, or incomplete stages in childhood development, there is a strong potential of an arrested development in emotional or social skills. What remains are the unmet emotional needs of childhood, tied to that specific age or developmental stage. It is likely that certain coping strategies were developed to help the child deal with their life crisis, which gets emotionally tied to a particular stimulus, such as being yelled at or physically threatened, and then stored away as an automatic reaction. This later continues to exist as a residual coping strategy and when activated, can pollute the thoughts and reactions of the adult psyche later in life, dredging up the past, activating latent fears, thoughts and behaviors which insert themselves into the present.

This transgression of the adult self by a childhood coping strategy contaminates any present sense of safety and emotional wellbeing, bringing instead strong emotional needs from the past which quickly override logic, higher reasoning, and relationship boundaries.

This contamination can easily subdue normal adult coping strategies and seize control of the moment. When activated, the inner child throws a tantrum demanding some resolution which is a hurt long past. The impact on the present can become toxic, leading to relationship harm or failure. The spontaneous contamination of your adult self by your inner child's need to assert control can result in illogical behavior or reactions. Sometimes, when you are reacting to a trigger, it is that inner child that is taking the wheel –taking control of where you go!

When your Inner Child Takes the Wheel

Watch out! That kid can't drive! Somehow in a moment of emotional defensiveness, your regressed child jumps up and grabs the wheel and starts to steer your emotions and reactions. The emotional car is crafted from beliefs, experiences, wounds, fears, assumptions, and body sensations.

When your inner child takes the wheel, he or she is unprepared for the complexities of navigating safely in an adult world and can fail to maintain healthy boundaries in adult relationships. The car goes quickly off course, mowing down the pedestrians in your life, damaging relationships, breaking boundaries, rules, often speeding headlong into a ditch of new wounds and hurt feelings.

If you are asking yourself *"why did this just happen"* after a reaction that came out of nowhere, you are not alone. Most adults will have moments when that annoying inner child makes itself known, seeking resolution for past hurts and unmet needs. It is looking to find resolution to some past injustice. It wants significance and cannot find it, so throws a tantrum when denied.

The inward experience of an active inner child hijacking you in the moment is confusing. It might seem like there is a true justification for the actions or words pouring out of you in that moment. However, the outward experience for others as they encounter your inner child seems illogical, irrational, even as manufactured drama. In fact, as it is happening you may be aware that you are being unfair to others or acting childish. But for the moment, you are an *observer*, as the inner child responds to its urgent need and powers your car with fear, anxiety, or anger. Like in a dream, you can only watch horrified as you speed out of control and mow down the people you love.

Signs of an Overactive Inner Child

While far from comprehensive, this list of warning signs includes the most typical experiences for those whose unrepaired past hurts or needs still resonate in their present lives. The behaviors and beliefs connected to these signs can destroy relationships and prevent the sufferer from achieving a sense of peace and stability in life, making navigating life exceedingly difficult. The key to unlocking and healing the inner child, and stopping his tantrums and rampages, is to look back into your personal history and see the patterns of hurt, disappointment, even traumas. This would include the intrusion of pornography and supernormal stimuli. To do this, you will need to take a deep dive into the past.

Inward Signs	**Outward Signs**
• Absolutist beliefs	• Addictions
• Accepting learned family dysfunctions	• Asserting power or control over others
• Discomfort with self-identity	• Codependency
• Emotionally blocked judgement	• Dramatic reactions
• Emotionally motivated	• Intimacy issues
• Fear for safety or wellbeing	• Irrational actions
• Feelings of emptiness	• Lack of basic trust
• Over Identification with others or status	• Lashing out at others
• Social anxiety.	• Shifting blame to others
• Unrelenting feelings of grief or loss	• Disregarding other's boundaries
	• Volatile relationships

Well known causes of an arrested inner-child

The Adverse Childhood Experiences (ACE)[10] study is one of the largest investigations of childhood abuse and neglect that links adult health and well-being. To read more about the ACE study:

https://www.cdc.gov/violenceprevention/aces/about.html

THE ACES QUIZ

Check the box for any of the following events if you experienced them before your 18th birthday:

☐ Did a parent or other adult in the household often or very often... Swear at you, insult you, put you down, or humiliate you? or Act in a way that made you afraid that you might be physically hurt?

☐ Did a parent or other adult in the household often or very often... Push, grab, slap, or throw something at you? Or, ever hit you so hard that you had marks or were injured?

☐ Did an adult or person at least 5 years older than you ever... Touch or fondle you or have you touch their body in a sexual way? Or attempt to, or actually have oral, anal, or vaginal intercourse with you?

☐ Did you often or very often feel that ... No one in your family loved you or thought you were important or special? or Your family didn't look out for each other, feel close to each other, or support each other?

☐ Did you often or very often feel that ... You didn't have enough to eat, had to wear dirty clothes, and had no one to protect you? Or your parents were too drunk or high to take care of you or take you to the doctor if you needed it?

☐ Were your parents ever separated or divorced?

☐ Was your mother or stepmother: Often or very often pushed, grabbed, slapped, or had something thrown at her? or sometimes, often, or very often kicked, bitten, hit with a fist, or hit with something hard? or ever repeatedly hit over at least a few minutes or threatened with a gun or knife?

☐ Did you live with anyone who was a problem drinker or alcoholic, or who used street drugs?

☐ Was a household member depressed or mentally ill, or did a household member attempt suicide?

☐ Did a household member go to prison?

Add up the number of boxes you checked. This is your ACE score. _____

While there is no absolute prediction of what will happen when you have a significant score, we do know the probability of negative outcomes increases as your total number of events rises. Porn addiction has not been studied as one of the outcomes of ACEs, yet other addictions and behavioral problems are quite common when ACEs are high. It would follow that if you have had certain ACE events, your likelihood of seeking solace, companionship, adventure, escape, stress relief and so on could be linked to porn addiction development. We do know that cybersexual addictions and social media addictions are often the result of a childhood that is disenfranchised or neglectful. Below is an excerpt from the ACE study that explains how they can help predict certain common reactions. Notice s\that high risk and addictive behaviors are well represented, as are emotional problems and life instability.

THE ALARMING RESULTS OF THE ACE STUDY

Only one-third in this study reported no adverse childhood experiences. Of the two-thirds of respondents who reported an adverse experience, 87 percent scored two or more. *One in six of all respondents had an ACE score of four or higher.*

THESE SCORES WERE THEN CORRELATED WITH EACH PARTICIPANT'S HEALTH PROBLEMS, REVEALING THE URGENCY WITH WHICH WE NEED TO ACT TO CREATE SAFE, RESPECTFUL, AND LOVING HOMES IN WHICH EVERYONE CAN THRIVE.

- More than half of those with ACE scores of 4 or higher reported having learning or behavioral problems at school.

- High ACE scores correlated with high workplace absenteeism, financial problems, and lower lifetime income.

- For those with an ACE score of 4 or more, depression was prevalent in 66 percent of women and 35 percent of men (compared with an overall rate of 12 percent with an ACE score of zero).

- There is a 5,000 percent increased likelihood of suicide attempts from zero to an ACE score of 6.

- Adults with an ACE score of 4 were seven times more likely to be an alcoholic.

- With an ACE score of 6 or more, the likelihood of IV drug use was 4,600 percent greater than for those with a score of zero.

- The prevalence of rape went from 5 percent with an ACE score of zero to 33 percent at a score of 4 or more.

- High risk behaviors predicted by the ACE score included smoking, obesity, unintended pregnancies, multiple sexual partners, and STDs.

- An ACE score of 6 or more produced a 15 percent or greater chance than those with a score of zero, of a person currently suffering from any of the leading causes of death in the United States: chronic obstructive pulmonary disease (COPD), ischemic heart disease, and liver disease. They were twice as likely to suffer from cancer, and 4 times as likely to have emphysema.

SOURCE: Bessel van der Kolk, M.D. (2014), *The Body Keeps the Score: Brain, Mind, and Body in the Healing of Trauma*, pp. 148-149.

The Deep Dive

"The past is already written. The ink is dry.[11]"

The deep dive is the foundation of your change towards the *bigger than porn* goal you will need to deactivate porn from your dopamine drive. Do not skip it, and do not minimize it. Do the work, painful or not, and you will find the rest falls into place. If you do not take the deep dive seriously, you will continue to struggle and may in all likelihood fail to break free.

I resist the temptation to offer too specific instructions to guide you because I want this to be personal. It will be unique to you. And if done correctly, it will not be fun. For most men it is about as easy as cliff diving, if you are afraid of both heights and water. This first step is not easy because it will provoke some anxiety. My best advice is to begin immediately and just do it. The plunge is scarier than actually hitting the water, and it will not take long for the anxiety or fear to vanish.

This deep dive will help you know what **mental fusions** or **neuropathways** have developed to hijack your mind and have taken your thoughts captive. Once you have that information, your battle plan to take your mind back can begin in earnest. If it helps, google *mental fusion* or *cognitive fusion* as well as *neuropathways*. These develop as we attach thought to experiences, sensations/feelings, and emotions. Beliefs are tied to our mental fusions, and they become the foundation for all of our behavioral decisions at one level or another.

"The unexamined life is not worth living" Socrates

Know yourself …take captive every thought to make it obedient to Christ. (2 Corinthians 10:5).

Do not conform to the pattern of this world but be transformed by the renewing of your mind. Then you will be able to test and approve what God's will is—his good, pleasing, and perfect will. (Romans 12:2).

What do these two scriptures tell us about the state of a man's mind? In its most simplistic form, our minds are conditioned by life in the presence of this world and the people around us, which in turn takes us off the intended path that God has for us. Therefore, we must make a conscious effort to renew our minds, to shake off the world's conditioning, and bring ourselves back into right standing with God in Christ. How do you do that? I have heard so many preachers my entire life throw these scriptures out, but seldom give a strategic plan to make it happen. So, let's begin by taking back at least one part of your life and mind, and renew it. Let's take back your sexual self-identity and healthy masculinity that was stolen from you in your youth.

The deep dive we are about to take is foundational in truly *winning the peace* while engaging in your battle with cybersexual temptation and addiction, as well as the tool we use to identify the origin of the *Hated Enemy*. Origin stories teach us why things are as they are in the present. By examining the beginning of your ill-chosen path, you can find the deviation from plan, and jump back to the correct path.

Choosing a path. I recall when I was young my family always watched the annual showing of the Wizard of Oz. Back then, all we ever saw was in black and white. When I was a few years older, at my grandparents' house with their color tv, I saw it for the first time in color. I noticed for the first time that the yellow brick road which spiraled out from "the beginning" had a red brick road that spiraled out with it, something that was not as pronounced in black and white. We are not told where this red road went, but in the movie, you could see it went mostly in the opposite direction. Dorothy was told to follow the yellow brick road to Oz and the solution to her problem, and not to leave it. Ever wonder where that other road led? I did. I asked my dad and he simply said, "someplace else, and that wasn't where she needed to be."

God has a path for all of us. This path will take us on a journey that, if followed, allows us to grow, overcome, and in the end, find our way home to him. But so many take that other road, like porn and drugs, selfishness, and greed. They quickly find that they are going in the wrong direction.

This Photo by Unknown Author is licensed under CC BY-SA-NC

If you notice, in the beginning of the spiral of those two brick roads, it would be easy to step from one to the other for a while, but then they part and go off in their own way, and you can no longer see one from the other.

As children, we start at the very center and are intended to follow a designated path. But for many, forces and choices take them along the wrong path early on, and soon they can no longer even see any alternatives.

Such is growing up male. We start off with wonderful potential to be compassionate, self-aware, open, and loving. But because males are also dualistic with aggressive self-determination, we easy fall into the wrong way of traveling through life. Human culture has recognized this truth since the beginning, and God in His wisdom gave us a mother and a father to guide us between the two sides of our male nature. Unfortunately, culture, weak parents, and mission drift has created poor boundaries in male development. In addition, negative and positive reinforcements are experienced that drive us to contain and manage masculinity into what each culture desires at any given time.

The Deep Dive Unpacked

To begin unlocking the mental fusions that drive your addictive reactions, our first and in some cases, most unpleasant task is to take a *deep dive* into the history of your own addiction development. We will be doing just that in several stages. This deep dive is designed to specifically root out where the timeline of your life deviated from the intended path.

This is something you will be doing on your own, and it is very private. I suggest you keep it that way as you work on it. It should be shared only with the group leader or your counselor/coach. If you want to discuss the particulars inside the group, go ahead. But you are not required to do so. Keeping it private helps you be more honest with yourself.

Most importantly, keep this private because, if you are married and in conflict over your porn history and usage, much of what you write could become a trigger for painful conversations leading to excessive defensiveness on your part. Remember, the past is already written, and you cannot defend it or change it. So, some things are better left alone until you and your wife are emotionally, psychologically, and spiritually ready to address the most difficult issues of intimate knowing.

The Deep Dive Process

- Think back on your childhood or teenage years. Find the first time you connected to sex through exposure to porn, abuse, or some other related event. Something that was external to your normal childhood imaginations.
- Use that event as ground zero and begin to create a timeline that tells the story of your progression from innocence to captivity. The addiction or the abuse you engage in has taken primacy in your life somewhere. Your quest is to find the progressions and the links.
- Once you have a basic timeline, go back, and see if there are any missing pieces or events that you left out. Your goal is a *thick description* of the events, not a cursory overview.
- Keep this information to yourself so you can openly examine all the parts without fear of being shamed in the eyes of your spouse or others.

- Once you have discovered the point where you actually see addiction or habitual abuse taking over, you have arrived.
- Now, take a step back mentally and find the pattern(s). Note them and define them the best you can.

If you are a template guy, google lifeline templates and get some ideas. Or use more primitive visual aids and chart it out on paper. Whatever works for you. But whatever you do, divide the line into two sides, one for developmental ages and events, like starting school, making a first friend, parents divorced, sibling events that affected you, etc. These are all on the "normal" side of life events.

On the opposite side, indicate when and how you began your journey into sexual awareness and self-identification as it connects to sex and belonging. E.g., saw a porn magazine, saw adults having sex, found that others did not like me, lost my friends, withdrew to cyber-life, gaming, or other isolation practices, discovered online porn, discovered masturbation, started to understand my own sexual identity, learned what other boys thought of me, etc.

Typical events that lead to porn and cyber-addiction might look the following:

- Discovered porn magazines or movies when I was __ years old and looked at them frequently.
- Was shown graphic porn movies by a friend, older child, or adult.
- Heard about porn from friends and searched the internet until I found it.
- Was molested by an older child or adult.
- Sexually acted out with friends, neighbors, or relatives.
- Was alone and lonely much of the time and felt disconnected from people or family.

- Found that porn gave me a special type of excitement.
- Began searching for more porn.
- Looked at porn with friends.
- Masturbated to porn for the first time or discovered masturbation as a result of watching porn.
- Masturbated or acted out porn scenes with friends or while watching with friends.
- Began planning to watch porn by looking for opportunities to be alone.
- Watched porn in the middle of the night so I would not get caught.
- Found relief from loneliness in porn.
- Fantasized about having the relationships I saw in porn because girls didn't notice me.
- Found myself recalling porn images when masturbating.
- Was unable to masturbate without porn frequently.
- Began viewing girls around me as sexual objects or opportunities.

Once you complete it, show it to your group coach for feedback if you are in the group. If not, review it with an accountability partner, or counselor. If you have none of these, you will be less likely to overcome your porn habit, but the tool can still help you. This is the foundation of your big self-examination in building a behavior chain and completing your addiction cycle worksheet. So, do not put it off, and don't minimize it. Do your deep dive now and do it with serious intent. This will be the foundation of understanding that will allow you to deconstruct your addiction and cycle and reconstruct your life going forward, so it needs to be completed and well understood before you move forward to your ultimate freedom from porn.

STOP HERE until you have completed the deep dive.

Your Experiences Made You as You Are Today

As you worked on your lifeline in the Deep Dive, no doubt you began to see some of the events and reasons why you think some of what you believe regarding porn, people, and yourself. You are beginning to see why your relationships are what they are, and why you are feeling what you are feeling. Before we get any deeper into your specific cycle deconstruction, I want you to take a pause and learn something new about your developmental programming running in the background.

We call this programming, *schemata*. Everyone has a collection of schemata that combine to create understanding and a working worldview which addresses *everything* we experience, think, feel, choose, and do in life. Schemata are the programs and subroutines of human thought. And, like any other operating code, they are programed in and can be either functional or dysfunctional. In this section, we are going to look at how eighteen common *irrational schemata* create dysfunction in relationships. But first, let us understand how schemata are created.

Jean Piaget[12] codified his theory of cognitive development in young children, describing a unique way of classifying and organizing knowledge. He describes the building blocks of understanding as units of knowledge that build one on top of the other to create understanding, even as data changes. He called these individual building blocks a schema, "a cohesive, repeatable action sequence possessing component actions that are tightly interconnected and governed by a core meaning"

(Piaget, 1952, p. 7). It goes something like this. A young child is given his first pet, a puppy. He learns that a puppy is a living animal, just like he is. A living animal is a schema. Then, a puppy, being different than a little boy modifies or accommodates added information, e.g., four legs, not two, a tail, fur, etc. That information is assimilated into a new schema "puppy." Now he has developed multiple schemata for living animals, boy and puppy. Later, when he first meets a cat, he might honestly declare it a puppy. But soon find it is differentiated from puppies in its sound, actions, claws, etc. He now has a schema for "cat." And his schemata combine to broaden his underlying schema of living animal to include cats as well as dogs and boys.

The brilliance of *schema as building blocks* theory is that all knowing can be constructed and deconstructed if we can only see the constituent parts clearly. The ability of human beings to have complex interactions with the world, and to anticipate and manipulate the future is enabled by our developmental capacity to accommodate and assimilate new knowledge, and to construct mental schemata, even to anticipate new schemata. Healthy functional schemata allow people to live healthy and functional lives. But consider what happens when the programming is flawed, and schemata are linking incorrectly, irrationally, or malignantly. This results in some maladaptive and irrational belief systems. Let us look at some common results of such poor programming.

Schema-Focused Relationships

A schema is a strongly held belief a person has developed about self, others, and the world. A schema, or schemata (plural) are amoral, neither caring about nor determined by moral certainty. They are what they are from experience, and therefore are assumed to be correct. Therefore, schemata can be positive or negative in how they affect a person without necessarily reflecting the moral character of the person. For instance, an abused child might be aggressive in nature, but is not necessarily a bad child, only a reactive one. Once a schema is accepted as necessary or true for an individual, their life will become governed by that schema in concert with others. Schemata allows all of us to navigate through life. However, faulty or irrational schemata create themes in thought, feelings, and behaviors that can become the source of major dysfunction. We see this most vividly in interpersonal relationships, particularly in marriage.

Faulty or irrational relationship-focused schemata set up patterns of interaction that can distort or damage intimate relationships. Healthy ones do the opposite. Understanding the full extent of schemata in your own life will be impossible. Many to most are established in early childhood, and then built upon continuously. It takes a lifetime to bring the major ones under control through understanding. Most modifications are made as we age and experience a wider variety of the variables of life. We call this maturing. But for all human beings, there will be underlying schemata that simply are, and we are being driven by them unaware. When those schemata are negative, the relationship we form with our own self and with others is also negative.

Psychologist Jeffrey Young defined eighteen common *negative schemata* which tend to develop early in life and affect future relationships. Young's Schema-Focused Relationship Checklist[13] is useful to understand how and why some relationships are prone to reactive behavior. Below is Young's list of common negative schemata with descriptions of beliefs that might be present and are guiding relational understanding.

Emotional Deprivation: My needs will never be met. (Nurture, empathy, and protection).

Abandonment/Instability: The expectation that others will not be there when you need them most. (Can be associated with loss through divorce, death, abandonment).

Mistrust/Abuse: The expectation of being hurt, manipulated, or exploited. (Can be from abusive parents, siblings, or others).

Social Isolation/Alienation: Fear of not fitting in or being different from peers. (Usually caused from early childhood experiences).

Defectiveness/Shame: The belief one is internally flawed and if someone gets close, they will discover this truth. Powerful sense of shame and vulnerable to criticisms.

Failure: The inability to perform as well as others, particularly peers, feeling untalented, inept, or stupid. (Tends to cause avoidance out of fear of failing).

Dependence/Incompetence: The belief that one is not capable of dealing with the demands of daily life.

Vulnerability to Harm and Illness: The expectation of harm or illness, often catastrophic in scope, making one overly cautious and self-protective.

Enmeshment/Undeveloped Self: Tends to be overly attached to others, with an inability to individuate from parents or to set appropriate boundaries. (A sense of depersonalization or undefined self apart from others).

Subjugation: Belief that one must submit to the control or will of others to be accepted or to avoid negative consequences.

Self-Sacrifice: Excessive drive to meet the needs of others at the cost of one's own needs or happiness.

Approval-Seeking/Recognition-Seeking: A dependence on the approval of others, one's self-esteem is linked to external approvals. Impaired limits and boundaries

Entitlement/Grandiosity: A belief that one should be able to have, do, or say what they want despite the effect it will have on others.

Insufficient Self-Control/Self-Discipline: The inability to tolerate frustration, with inability to restrain emotions or the expression of impulses or feelings.

Emotional Inhibition: Repression and inhibition of emotion in order to avoid rejection by others.

Unrelenting Standards/Hyper criticalness: High internal drive and demand for competence, achievement, rule-following, ethics, and efficiency to avoid criticism. Must work harder.

Punitiveness: The belief that people (including self) should be punished harshly for their mistakes.

Negativity/Pessimism: A pervasive expectation and focus on the negative outcomes in life and/or minimizing the positives.

All have been affected by the past, and many if not most of us have dealt with reactions that could very well be connected to one of these misbeliefs. While that is normal, living a life bound by these misbeliefs is not. I refer to these beliefs as *misbeliefs* for a reason. While on the surface, and through the lens of loss, abuse, or misfortune they may look reasonable or rational, they are not. A misbelief is an irrational belief that causes someone to act in a way that is debilitating or disruptive to their best life.

Irrational beliefs (misbeliefs) are identifiable when you write them down and then look more closely. Typically, an irrational belief has two parts, one that sets up the belief and may in fact be true or rational, then a second part that is not actually true, but sounds true. A classic example of an irrational belief is: "I do not have the love I want in my life because I am not a loveable person." If the first part is true, that this person does not have the love of their life, then it is rational. That is a fact at the moment. What makes it irrational is the second part that offers a false conclusion; that they are therefore not loveable.

Often, in an irrational belief we can see it is irrational because of the absolute nature of the belief. In this case, that the person is unlovable. That is stated as an absolute, but how can that be known? Just because someone does not feel love in the moment does not mean they never can.

Refuting an irrational belief is the primary method used in Cognitive Behavioral Therapy techniques. Finding the irrational part of any belief allows the individual to re-frame their belief and to alter their interpretation of events. Once that happens, the feelings associated with that event will undoubtedly change. Once feelings change, the choices for action, the coping strategies, also change. Behavior follows feelings-based decisions, so necessarily outcomes are changed.

One client once insisted that "he must be gay," even though he was married to a woman he sincerely loved and was attracted to sexually and emotionally and had fathered five children with her over there ten years of happy marriage. He was convinced he must be gay because in his early childhood, starting around age six, he was repeatedly molested by an older cousin until he was about thirteen when the cousin went off to college.

He reported that he hated molestation, and the way it felt dirty and how he felt used. But, because his body responded to the sexual stimuli, and because over the years he began to actively engage in sexual participation with that abuser, that he *must have* "wanted it, and enjoyed it." This, of course, is a faulty schema. He did experience sexual abuse, his body did respond, and he did become habituated to gay sex for a time. Compounding this misperception was an awakened curiosity about sex and gay porn as his porn addiction developed. Despite the occasional revisiting of his about through compulsions to view gay porn at times, his fundamental sexual attraction was heterosexual, and remained so. The irrational belief or schema that developed was *if you enjoyed or responded to the gay sex, it must be because he was gay.* He took a long time to realize that this was not rational, and was in fact, absolutist thinking.

I have told many of my clients who hold distorted views of life or self through irrational beliefs they are *looking into a faulty mirror*. We all rely on mirrors to reflect to us a representation of ourselves in life. How others react or respond to us is the evidence we rely on to know if we are received well or correctly. Our actions are heavily determined by how we perceive the world's reaction to us. But people make poor mirrors. Many are cracked, offering fragmented views of how they experience us. Others are dirty or scratched, obliterating much of the detail. Still others are like funhouse mirrors, warped and distorted. Our self-beliefs are susceptible to these faulty reflections, and over time can become so damaged that we hold misbeliefs as truth.

Once a negative schema or misbelief takes hold, relationships are altered. Imagine trying to have a relationship with someone that makes you feel unworthy, shame filled, or defective. If that person were a constant in your life, you would begin to react negatively toward them. That reaction could be to treat them badly, or it could be to absorb their views and treat yourself badly.

Eventually, you will find a new way to cope. Many do this with distractions that allow them to escape the present in favor of a fantasy they can control. This is why pornography, gaming, and other cyber world activities are so alluring. The person can control the environment, interact through an avatar or through fantasy, and have little to no negative interactions. If it gets boring or unpleasant, the variables can be changed in the moment, or the person can simply quit and do something else. Escaping a negative world, fostered by misbeliefs, seems to be one of the most common reasons I see many of my clients engaging in cyber-sexual activities.

Beyond addictions, misbeliefs also influence the primary relationships between people. If you think about it, you can see your own reasoning in how you react to others. Take parents for instance. When a small child is demanding attention, a parent will respond with super-patience most of the time. This is simple due to a schema attached to parenting. "My child needs me to help him, he cannot do this for himself yet. It is my job to help him." This is an automatic thought. You are unlikely to be aware that it is activated when your child needs something. You simply act on it. Most all schemata work this way, as a subroutine that is automatic. Your interactions with a spouse, parent, boss, friend, and others are all based on schemata. Most are functional and rational. But some are not. Examining your own schemata allows you to unlock the hidden subroutines and modify them for more effective responding.

Schemata also develop to help navigate the unpleasantries of life. There are many things in life that hurt us, or that might hurt us. In the physical world, we learn not to touch the stove, not to stick things into light sockets, and never to run with scissors. But in the world of human interaction, we must learn many more variables. The world is full of good people and bad, and most of all, people that fall somewhere in between and are unpredictable at times. Pain avoidance develops as we encounter people, places, and things that cause or threaten to cause harm. This natural process sets up the rules of survival in our belief system. But the unpredictability of people, and the lack of sophisticated or informed thoughts of childhood lay down a lot of faulty rules. These rules get carried through to adulthood. Much like the inner child driving the emotional car we discussed earlier, faulty, or protective schemata develop in youth and drive immature behavioral choices.

Now that you have a basic understanding of how and why schemata matter in your own life, review the list of eighteen faulty relationship schemata once more. Look carefully this time. Which ones are active in your own life? Use these in your quest to unlock meanings in the upcoming behavior chaining process you will construct. You will be surprised just how mistaken many of your thoughts and reactions are when it comes to navigating the day-to-day events associated with people and your inner child.

The Behavior Chain

Knowing yourself is the first major step in taking your thoughts captive (2 Cor 10:15), and then transforming them to conform to the mind and image of Christ (Rom 12:2). We begin this vital step with an exploration of self, using a time-tested tool, the Behavior Chain. Behavior chaining is a behavior modification process that uses cognitive behavioral theory to understand why someone does what they do, challenge the beliefs and feelings that drive negative behavior, and then to find alternative behavioral responses.

If you look back earlier in our process to part one and the Loss of Self, you will recall that choices define the behavioral process. Cognitive Behavioral Theory is the most often applied counseling theory for helping people change unwanted behavior. Recalling the choice cycle from earlier, we can start to apply some of what you have already learned about your own self by working through your personal cause and effect processes. In that work, you will:

Identify and understand your behavior/addiction cycle, giving you the power and opportunity to break it for good.

Construct a relapse prevention plan to keep you from using porn as a medication for your unwanted feelings.

Construct a relapse recovery plan to help you get back on track if you fail to stay sober.

Learn how to explain to your wife or others what is happening so that they can understand, empathize, and help you overcome the pull of the cycle in the months to come.

Your cycle begins with the exposures you have had in life. Early childhood events are most powerful in setting up some automatic thinking, but more recent events are also powerful. Traumatic events, losses, and romantic failures can alter a person's belief system, which in turn directly impacts what that person will think about any given event that is related to that belief. From there the cycle continues, limited now by the choices that the belief (schema) has predetermined to by the appropriate ones.

To understand your **Personal Cognitive-Behavioral Cycle** (Figure 3), you will use the behavior chaining process to

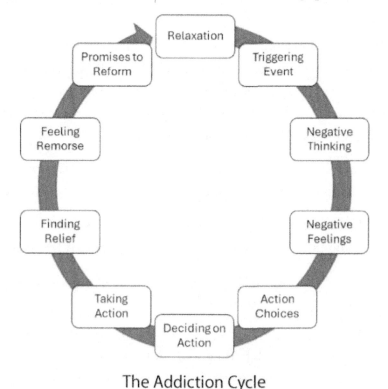

The Addiction Cycle
FIGURE 3: PERSONAL COGNITIVE-BEHAVIORAL CYCLE / ADDICTION CYCLE

establish a knowable behavior cycle specific to your addiction-driven behavior. By analyzing the completed behavior chain, you will be able to plug the findings (data) into the Addiction Cycle corresponding to the steps in the cycle.

Lapse Versus Relapse

Different programs define a lapse and a relapse differently. For our purposes, and to make it truly clear when the line has crossed, we will define our terms as follows:

Sobriety means not using and being consciously aware that you are not choosing to use.

Lapse means that you are thinking about using, dwelling on or fantasizing about using, lying, or other progression towards violating sobriety.

Relapse begins when you take any actions to make using likely. This includes planning and creating opportunities as well as actual use. For example, if you were an alcoholic, lapse would be thinking about or yearning for a drink. Relapse begins the moment you pick up your car keys planning to drive to get a drink somewhere. Or perhaps, lapse is thinking about a drink, relapse is searching the sofa, the house, the laundry for enough spare change and money to be able to buy a drink. Think of porn addiction the same way.

Constructing your Behavioral Chain

Before proceeding to build your behavior chain, you will need to gain some understanding into what constitutes a *thick description* of your actions, thoughts, and feelings which define your unique chain of behavior. It is this level of detail that will allow you to gain the necessary insight to unlock your cycle and begin breaking your current addiction or abuse chain.

The following "instructions" are intended to clarify the purpose, method, and relevant content of the behavior chain you are about to construct. The instructions are prepared as an overview, not a step-by-step method. For the actual construction of the chain, you may be given instructions to accomplish this task by your coach or in group.

While this worksheet describes the chain in a chronological order (start to finish description of the problem behavior), you may be asked by your coach or counselor to construct your chain in *reverse chronology*, beginning at the end result, and constructing the precipitating thoughts, feelings, and events that preceded the final outcome. This reverse order actually makes the analysis process easier, and yields a more detailed account, and can help you develop a keen understanding of your actual trigger(s).

To build a thick description you will:

1. **Describe the specific action, feeling, or thoughts associated with the targeted (problem) behavior. Be extremely specific and detailed. No vague terms.**
   - Identify exactly what you did/said, thought, and felt and when needed for clarity of context, what others did or said.
   - Describe the intensity of the behavior and other characteristics of the behavior that are important when needed to help you and your counselor/coach understand important context.
   - Describe the problem behavior in enough detail that an actor in a play or movie could recreate the behavior exactly.

2. **Describe the specific PRECIPITATING EVENT** that started the whole chain of behavior. This would be the triggering event. Examples could be getting yelled at by someone, ignored, left out of something, criticized, etc. Start with the environmental event that started the chain, even if it does not seem to you that the event "caused" the problem behavior. E.g., *"I came home from work to an empty house."*

Questions to get at this are:

- What exact event precipitated the start of the chain reaction?
- When did the sequence of events that led to the problem behavior begin? When did the problem start?
- What was going on the moment the problem started?
- What were you doing, thinking, feeling, imagining at that time?
- Why did the problem behavior happen on that day instead of the day before?

3. **Describe VULNERABILITY FACTORS** you can identify as happening before the precipitating event. What factors or events made you more vulnerable to a problematic chain? Areas to examine are:
   - Physical illness; unbalanced eating or sleeping; injury.
   - Use of drugs or alcohol, misuse of prescription drugs
   - Stressful events in the environment (either positive or negative)
   - Intense emotions, such as sadness, anger, fear, loneliness
   - Previous behaviors of your own that you found stressful.

4. **Describe in excruciating detail THE CHAIN OF EVENTS** that led up to the problem behavior. Imagine that your problem behavior is chained to the precipitating event in the environment.

How long is the chain? Where does it go? What are the links? Write out all links in the chain of events, no matter how small. Be specific, as if you are writing a script for a play.

- What exact thought(s) or belief, feeling, or action followed the precipitating event? What thought, feeling, or action followed that? What next?
- For each link in the chain, is there is a smaller link I could describe. For example, is there a detail that contributes to this link before or after that needs to be added or included? The links can be thoughts, emotions, sensations, and behaviors.

Drafting your Chain

It is likely that as you complete step one, you will begin to feel uncomfortable with yourself as you identify your negative behaviors. This is normal. Seeing yourself from the outside causes you to evaluate your behaviors more clearly. Sometimes examining past behaviors will trigger guilt and shame, or even disgust and self-loathing. Hang on to this experience because it can help you when you need to be empathetic to your spouse when she experiences or remembers your behavior.

To begin your behavior chain, you first need a sense of what it is you want to explore. You have two primary choices:

Option 1. Describe and analyze your *typical* behavior as it relates to cybersex or sexual addiction, or

Option 2. Describe and analyze a *major event* that impacted your life, like getting caught again, and your wife moving out, or being fired and relapsing completely.

Option one is the most viable choice for someone who has a consistent pattern and no major defining events or long-term breaks with intensive relapses. Option two works well for those whose addictive behavior is tied to one-time events, spousal discoveries, or another major event, without habitual acting out in between. An example of a more isolated event might be that you have been overly candid and needy with a coworker and your spouse has discovered it. The choice is yours but consider where your biggest risk exists and choose to work in that area.

Once you have selected what to analyze, you will first create a brief description to frame the story you are telling. Imagine that you are a writer, and you want to sell a producer on your next screenplay. First you would give him a brief overview of the story. For this example, you will draft a short paragraph or two that does just that. We will call this our screenplay proposal.

Screenplay Proposal Example:

> *"When I become frustrated with my life, I find relief by finding a private place and surfing for porn videos. When I do this, I look through a number of sites and save tabs of interesting items until I find the one that is most exciting. Then I use that video to excite myself and masturbate until I get released. Afterwards, I usually become relaxed and less frustrated, but I also feel guilty or shameful. I tell myself I will not do it again, and then I can relax because the guilt goes away when I imagine myself porn free."*

Storyboards are used in screenwriting to work out the sequence and details for movies. In our case, you will write a narrative that breaks the action into *camera checkable moments*, so that an actor could accurately play the part of you when using porn. This narrative storyboard is used to describe the actions, the thoughts, and the feelings that occur leading up to and through your use of porn. Developing your storyboard begins with the "action" thread of your movie. The behavior chain is a narrative version of a screenplay storyboard in many ways.

In a typical storyboard, you would describe the scene in enough detail to convey to an actor what is to take place, offering up a word picture that allows others to imagine the scene with clarity. It should follow the basic story you described in your screenplay proposal, revising as needed, with moment-by-moment detail for each frame of the action.

Camera checkable means what a camera would see if you were taking still photos of an event. Each frame of a movie is a single picture that when connected in sequence, becomes a motion picture. In your action sequence, you will write brief statements that describe the action that a camera would see. If you are stating a thought, belief, feeling, or sensation, you do not want to put it into this column. Just actions that can be photographed.

Step 1-Actions

Completing column one: These *action frames* are to be depicted in a 3-column table, in column number one, the Actions column (see example below). This column depicts a progression of visible or discernable actions step by step. For each change in the action, a new table cell is added. You will have twenty-five to fifty entries to describe the action events in your typical behavior cycle. Do not worry about columns two or three yet; just do the actions for column one.

Once you have finished the action column, read it aloud in reverse order. The reason for this is to see if it makes sense. If while reading in reverse the steps seem to leave out details on how the steps are connected, you need to thicken your narrative with more details. For instance, if I asked you how you got to work today, and you said, "I drove my car" that would technically be true, but if I wanted to repeat your actions, I would need to know what kind of car, did you drive alone or carpool, what route did you take, etc. Remember, a thick description means to *"characterize the process...paying attention to contextual detail in observing and interpreting..."[14]*

Once you have completed your column one action content, share it with your coach to see if he identifies any missing parts. Once he and you agree that the description is good, you can proceed to step two. If there are missing parts, add them before proceeding to part two.

Step 2-Thoughts

Completing column two. This next step is much easier than step one because you will only be adding the thoughts and feelings associated with the actions you have already described. This takes less self-confrontation than your exploration of your visible behavior; it is your direct behavior that tends to be the source of most shame. What you see others experiencing about you triggers higher levels of shame and avoidance in you than your thought processes. However, it is your inner processing of thoughts and feelings that prompt or support your behavioral choices—they are directly connected.

Your task now is to review your actions as listed in column two and three, one line at a time, to recall the thoughts and feelings connected with each individual action. List those thoughts and feelings as you remember them at the time they occurred. Resist the urge to explain or justify your past behavior or processes.

Thoughts can be reactive. If someone hits you, you get angry and can go immediately to *fight-or-flight* responding, hardly thinking, but know that an action is warranted. Think carefully about what you were thinking and why you came to any conclusions between thought and action as you complete column two.

Column two describes your self-talk (as best as you can recall it) which triggered your feelings and behavioral choices, or that were reinforced by your actions. Beliefs are thoughts and are often connected to automatic triggers which control feelings and actions. For instance, feeling lonely, unappreciated, or abandoned can be connected to established beliefs that you are unlovable or somehow not worthy of connection to other people. As you go line by line in describing your recalled actions, list any thoughts you recall connected to that event in column in column two.

Step 3-Feelings.

Completing column three. Feelings can be connected to something you want to achieve, which results in feelings like pleasure, excitement, guilt, anger, or they can be feelings of anticipation, like excited, aroused, curious, horny. Feelings can also be negative because of behavior or thoughts which you want to eliminate, such as loneliness, anger, guilt, shame, frustration. Whatever the connected feeling is, the thought will connect as well. You can list more than one thought or feeling with each event.

If the thought led to the feeling, and the feeling led to the action, write it that way. For instance, thinking you are abandoned can cause you to feel lonely, which in turn can cause you to seek out companionship. This is thought-feeling-action orientation.

If the action led to a feeling which creates or reinforces an established thought, you would write it that way. For instance, if you recently met a new person that makes you feel accepted, you might choose to remain close to them, which increases your feeling of acceptance and companionship, which tells you that you are not lonely. This is action-feeling-thought orientation.

EXAMPLE OF A COMPLETED BEHAVIOR CHAIN

Column 1: Action	Column 2: Thought	Column 3: Feeling
I came home to a messy house and my wife was asleep on the couch.	I work hard and she is not helping me. I believe that she just uses me, so she doesn't have to work.	I'm frustrated, angry, disappointed, and feeling unloved.
Decide to masturbate to porn.	I need to do something to get away from my negative feelings.	Frustrated, stressed, sad, or angry.

Wait until the conditions were ideal.	Can't do it until everyone is asleep.	Nervous, anxious.
Finish homework or chores or take time to myself watching TV or surfing Facebook.	Need to do something to occupy my time until everyone is asleep.	Nervous, anxious.
Make sure the coast is clear, that my wife and child are asleep.	I can't get caught.	Nervous, guilty, sad.
Set things up so that I don't get caught if either wake up: make it look like I am working on homework (or doing anything other than porn).	I can't get caught.	Nervous, worried, guilty.
Decide where to watch porn while avoid getting caught – couch, kitchen table, bathroom, or in office upstairs.	Where will I be least likely get caught?	Nervous, guilty.
Have an alibi in place: working on homework, paying bills, playing video games.	If my wife wakes up and asks what I am doing, what do I tell her to avoid getting caught.	Deceitful

Get ideas on what to masturbate to from something I see on TV, Facebook, website, or YouTube.	What kind of porn do I want to masturbate to tonight?	Excited, creative, imaginative.
Decide on what I will masturbate to.	N/A	Excited, creative, imaginative.
Get on my computer.	Time to get on the computer.	Excited.
Set up more alibis: email, Facebook, news, YouTube.	In case my wife wakes up, I can't just have porn sites open on my computer.	Nervous, worried.
Open webpage and begin searching porn.	Time to start surfing porn.	Excited, happy.
Access a porn site, begin looking at thumbnail links to videos of women having sex.	Time to find some videos to watch.	Excited, happy.
Pick a video to watch.	This video looks good.	Aroused.
Skip intro, go to first sexual act.	Intro = boring! Need to get to the good stuff.	Aroused, impatient.

Begin to rub myself through my pants a little, to get a good erection going.	I like what I am seeing.	Aroused, feels good.
Scan through the video, stopping at sex scenes/act, looking for more stimulation.	I want to see more, does the video get better?	Excited, hopeful.
Rub myself some more.	(Seeing more video) – Hot!	More intense arousal.
Check out the final climax of the video.	How does the video finish?	Aroused, excited, anxious.
Repeat with other videos, saving the videos that I may want to masturbate and climax to.	I need to check out other videos to see if I can find a better video to masturbate/climax to.	Aroused, excited, curious.
Take my penis out so I can masturbate better, but not too much because I want to save the climax for the best video I can find.	Time to get a little more serious about masturbating.	Need for more intense arousal/sensation.
Get about 8-12 tabs open with the videos I like the most for the night.	Need to find a few more videos I like.	Need for more intense arousal/sensation.

Stop searching for more videos.	I've spent enough time looking for new videos.	Tired/fatigued, saturated.
Begin narrowing down the videos.	Time to figure out which video I want to climax to.	Aroused, excited, picky/selective.
Bounce back and forth between videos, deleting the videos that I don't want to finish with, while masturbate just enough to keep me close to the edge.	Need to narrow down the videos.	Aroused, ready to finish.
Narrow the videos down to 2-3.	Need to narrow down the videos.	Intensely aroused, ready to finish.
Bounce between the remaining videos, figure out which one I want to watch while finishing, all while masturbate to maintain erection just short of climax.	Which of the 2-3 videos do I want to watch while finishing?	Intensely aroused, ready to finish.
Choose the video I want to climax to.	Need to pick the best video.	Intensely aroused, happy, excited.
Choose which part of the video I want to climax to.	Need to determine the best part of the	Intensely aroused, happy,

	video to watch while finishing.	excited, prepared.
Let my self-control go – masturbate vigorously to the video.	Time to finish!	Ready, happy, excited to finish.
Get ready to orgasm while watching the part of the video I picked to finish with. Have hand towel ready.	This is going to be awesome.	Awesome.
Stand up for a better climax (sometimes).	N/A.	N/A.
Get my hand towel ready.	N/A.	N/A.
Climax – sexual release.	Yes!	Euphoric.
Wrap my penis in the hand towel, collapse into the chair, eyes closed, thinking only about the effects of the climax and how good it feels.	Wow that was good.	Euphoric, relieved, happy.
Close web browser, clear my history, clean myself up, get dressed.	Ok, time to make like "it never happened."	Accomplished, but a little melancholy, hopeful that I

		will feel better after I get rid of the "evidence."
Go back to watching TV, doing homework, or surfing the net in an effort to forget about it.	There, all done, and nobody is the wiser.	Half accomplished and relieved, half guilty and unhappy with what I did.
Go to bed.	I've got to stop this. I need to say no to myself next time and come up with a better way to get my release.	More shame/guilt, sadness, frustration/anger with myself.

Once this table is completed, it's time to share it with a coach, counselor, or accountability partner.

Do not proceed to part three until you have reviewed your completed three column narrative with someone appropriate and have considered their input.

You need this outsider perspective to help determine if there are any omissions or missed opportunities for discovery. Only then should you continue to the next step, analyzing your chain...

Analyzing Your Chain

Now that you and your coach are satisfied that the chain is complete, you will start your analysis. This part is subjective to your content. The goal is to see *patterns* of thought, feeling, or behavior which are tied to your trigger(s) so that you can begin to disconnect them.

To accomplish this, read the entire chain, and on a separate sheet, list or highlight all the feeling words that you see, and try to connect them to specific actions. This is the process of deductive coding of your data set (the chain). It leads you from information to pattern identification, to a hypothesis of your process, to the theory of your addiction. Do not overthink this, it is really not that hard. Follow the procedure below for guidance and soon you can code this chain completely without much fuss.

1. Start with broad *categories* in mind I like to start with the feelings. In a behavior chain, feelings are **key *indicators*** because it is how we feel about what happened (usually filtered through our schemata) that tells us what we can or should do about it. Remember, thoughts are initially triggered by an event, and feelings follow those thoughts based on what we have experienced in the past. So, feelings are *drivers* in any addiction cycle. See if there are any repeating feelings, like anger, frustration, loneliness, etc. List out all the feeling words in your chain, and if repeated, weight by including hash marks in to indicate the number of times you see that feeling come up. This way you can quickly identify the dominant feelings in your pattern. Dominant feelings will give you a clue about what your macro-cognitions are that drive your conscious or subconscious thoughts.

2. Types and Kinds of feelings. Once you have all the feelings identified, group them by *types and kinds*. These descriptors, types and kinds, are classifications I use to help me see patterns. I use **types** to indicate the feeling groups (clusters) based on the primary feelings of anger, sadness, happiness, etc. and I use **kinds** to separate inward-focused feelings (aimed at self) and outward-focused feelings (projected at others). You can call them what you want to.

Remember, the goal is to find *patterns,* so, while the nuance is important, the patterns will come into focus easier when simplified. Feelings can be grouped into *types*, like **anger:** mad, frustrated, enraged, bitter, etc. to help identify patterns of a predominant type. *Kinds* help you to see if you are soaking in those feelings as an *inward* focus (lonely, scared, bored) versus projecting or aggressing as an *outward* focus (vengeful, angry, cheated, judged, ignored). When combined with actions and thoughts these clusters of feelings become *themes*. Grouping by types and kinds will begin to bring the pattern to the surface to move on to themes.

3. Collapse your listed feelings into primary feelings. We waited until now to further collapse back into primary feelings so that you might have a clear view of the nuances. Once that is accomplished, we need to simplify the feelings so that you can work with the data without too much noise. Using your list of types collapse the grouped feelings into primary (if possible) feelings. If you do not know what a *primary feeling* is, versus a secondary or nuanced feeling, reference the feelings chart below. In the center circle are the more primary feelings. Each ring outward is more nuanced.

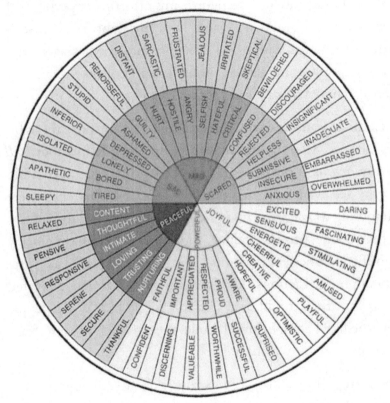

IMAGE CREATIVE COMMONS, CC BY-ND 2.0

In the center of the wheel are the primary feelings: *sad, mad, scared, peaceful, powerful, joyful.* Each ring outward is more nuanced as they extend from the primary feeling. Once you group your feelings, you can categorize them if you need to collect *types* and *kinds* of feelings together. Remember, the goal is to find patterns. Feelings that are similar, like anger: mad, frustrated, enraged, bitter, etc. indicate a pattern of kind. Types might be inward focused (lonely, scared, bored) versus outward focused (cheated, judged, ignored) feelings.

Look for the same clusters or patterns in your thought column. Do you see any related thoughts? (e.g., she is judging me, my boss does not recognize my effort). Or perhaps "I work hard and deserve…" and "it is my right to…" Just as with feelings, you can group thoughts into themes as well, if you see any. Group similar thoughts and collapse them into themes where you can and list them.

4. Look at your actions. This will take a little more thought. Try to see what your actions represent. Remember, **_all behavior has a purpose_**. It just needs to be examined a bit. Try to see what your actions *represented* or what they were attempting to *mitigate*. This is easier if you consider the actions as they connect to the feelings and thoughts you have already identified. Themed actions are best viewed as pre-programmed reactions. Like an autopilot that gets activated when you are in trouble. An example might be, "When people treat me like I am a failure, I panic, then get defensive to push their opinion away from me."

If you are, for instance, cold to your wife after an argument, it likely is because you want her to notice you are upset. This behavior is designed to send a message.

Finding the behavioral meaning might be tricky because we don't always accept or admit our behavior is there to communicate a message. We hide the reasons in blanket beliefs like, "*If someone makes me mad, of course I'm going to be touchy for a while. Everybody knows that normal.*" The reality is, this is more likely a way to manipulate the person you are mad at into acknowledging your pain and an attempt to make them come to the table and make amends.

When working on reasons behind behaviors, sometimes it is easier if you consider the actions as they connect to the feelings and thoughts you have already identified. Many times, action follows the feelings, and are reinforced by your thoughts. Other times, actions precede feelings, but are still likely based on thoughts.

When I am working with a client individually, I can ask him to describe his *here-and-now* awareness of what he is experiencing. But when you do this alone, it is up to you to try and be aware of yourself as you are viewing your patterns when they begin to emerge. It is helpful to record all of your *in the moment* thoughts and feelings that are happening while you are analyzing your data on a separate piece of paper. This would be a *field note*, something that you notice while researching, and want to come back to later. The client who gave me permission to use his behavior chain (heavily redacted) for the example chain in this book put it this way,

> *"When I started this process, I really thought I had control over the porn, and just needed to stop it with some tools. But as I looked at my patterns of behavior, thought, and feelings, it was like I was detached and hovering above my own self. I saw how much planning and scheming it took to just view porn in one sitting. Managing my environment, planning my excuses, looking out for my wife so I did not get caught, clearing history, and on and on. Suddenly, I realized for the first time that I do not have control over porn at all. It completely controls me. I think about it long before I start using, and it affects me all the time."*

This paragraph demonstrates a keen here and now revelation of his feelings, as he was exploring the past through his behavior chain. This would be a great field note to have for later in his case, as he overcomes his temptations, or when he is explaining his struggle to his spouse.

5. Identify major patterns across all three domains, action, thoughts, and feelings. Look to the thoughts to see if the thoughts caused the actions, or the actions were there to reinforce a thought (or belief), or the action was to appease or stop any feelings (most common). Make any notes that will help you to keep these discoveries in mind so that you can be mindful of them as you continue in your recovery process.

6. Construct a behavior cycle, or in most cases, an addiction cycle case presentation (see worksheet and example). Start by taking the information in your chain, plus your notes, and using this to fill in the boxes around the circle of the cycle below. You may choose to do this as bullet points on a separate paper first, to organize your thoughts.

The Addiction Cycle

The Addiction cycle is a graphic representation of the process you have uncovered in your behavior chain exercise. The cycle graphic allows you to plug in the components in the order that they occur and see the connection between events-thoughts-feeling-choices, etc. understanding the cycle graphic is straight forward.

One of my professors in research methodology called this type of work, *plug and chug*. Basically, you are taking information or *data points* from one format and plugging it into a form or graphic. That is what we are doing this week. Plug and chug the column data as stages of your cycle. For this you will identify the relevant data points from your coded behavior chain and list them together, then plug them into the cycle. Many are repetitive, so you can aggregate them as needed. If you have more than one negative thought connected with a negative event, you can label them 1,2, 3 etc. then in proceeding boxes, use those numbers to connect the feeling, actions, etc. to the specific negative thoughts as needed.

If you are having trouble finding the content for each box, review your chain to see if there are missing parts. Except for Boxes 8 & 9, all boxes *will* have content. Only a small minority of men will not have content in 8 or 9, so don't skip these, and

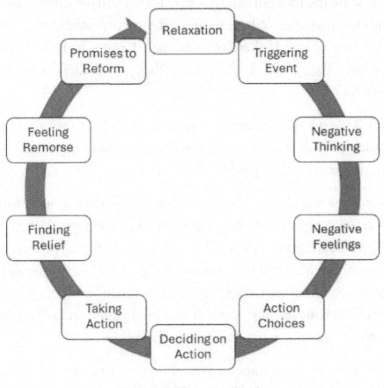

The Addiction Cycle

if you do, be prepared to explain yourself to your coach, counselor, or group because it is rare.

Starting clockwise at 12 o'clock, the cycle begins when you are in a state of relaxation (hopefully) and become triggered by a negative event at the 1:00 position. The cycle progresses in a predictable

Box 1 is the triggering event and the environment in which it occurred. What triggering event(s) did you identify in your chain? You may have only one, you may have several of them. E.g., "My wife was in a bad mood when I came home and got on me about minor things as if I were a failure."

Box 2 are the thoughts and/or beliefs that you have associated with the trigger(s). What are those thoughts / beliefs for each triggering event? If there is more than 1 event in Box 1, you will likely have more than one set of thoughts/beliefs activated as well.

Box 3 are the feelings that connect the thoughts to your action choices. What are the primary feelings connected to each of the triggering events listed?

Box 4 are the choices that you typically consider in an effort to resolve negative feelings; choices that are typical of you when you are in your cycle. These are often habitual, practiced, and automatic without much thought in the moment. However, your metacognition will tell you what they are. Based on your feelings, what choices did your mind offer you to combat any negative feelings or thoughts?

Box 5 is the set-up action you chose or typically choose to make the action possible. E.g., find an excuse to spend alone time so you can search the web for porn. Actions are based on the choices you made to alleviate your stress or distress from the thought/feeling event. I call this the setting up reactive action because those choices can be varied. (E.g., did you isolate yourself, seek opportunities to use, argue with your spouse so she would withdraw, storm out of the house so you could act out, etc.). What set up actions did you take to allow you freedom or opportunity to use porn?

Box 6 is the actual process of hunting and satisfying yourself in whatever manner you described. E.g., browsed sites while self-stimulating until you came to a point of saturation and settled on a specific video, then masturbated to orgasm. What did you do?

Box 7 is the immediate experience of relief, e.g., reaching a climax, swapping a pic, having sex, etc. and the thoughts associated with the relief. What happened that gave you a sense of relief or distraction from your negative events? What feelings or thoughts did that relief produce in you in that moment of relief?

Box 8 is where you likely (but not necessarily) experienced remorse, guilt, shame, or other negative consequences after the immediacy of relief has passed. If nothing negative was experienced, you may have been in denial, or you may have a belief that supports your choices that would be associated with narcissistic traits. How did you feel once your actions were completed when you thought about what you had just done, and the events that led you there?

Box 9 is your attempt to relieve yourself of any negative feelings about your action, such as promising yourself this was the last time, asking God to heal you, or other ways of convincing yourself you are ok. Did you tell yourself anything, make any promises, or use any other tactic to help you find relief from any guilt you felt because of your actions? If so, what was it?

Completing your cycle requires that you now take the identified data points from your coded behavior chain and plug them into the cycle. Many are repetitive, so you can aggregate them as needed. If you have more than one negative thought connected with a negative event, you can label them 1, 2, 3 etc. then in proceeding boxes, use those numbers to connect the feeling, actions, etc. to the specific negative thoughts as needed.

Addiction Cycle Worksheet

Box 1: Triggering Event	Box 6: Taking Action
Box 2: Negative Thoughts	Box 7: Finding Relief

Box 3: Negative Feelings	Box 8: Feelings of Remorse
Box 4: Response Choices	Box 9: False Promises
Box 5: Setup Action	Relaxation: Returning to your comfort zone...

If you are having trouble finding the content for each box, review your chain to see if there are missing parts. With the exception of boxes 8 & 9, all the boxes **will have** content. Only a small minority of men will not have content in 8 or 9.

Once this cycle graphic is complete, take time and review it with your coach. If you don't have a coach, review it with your accountability partner. (*IF* you don't have an accountability partner, you didn't complete the first vital assignment and you are not likely to succeed, so go back and find one). With the

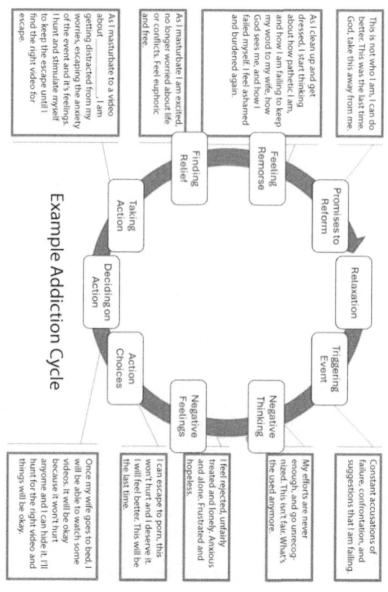

Example Addiction Cycle

This is not who I am. I can do better. This was the last time. God, take this away from me.

As I clean up and get dressed, I start thinking about how pathetic I am, and how I am failing to keep my word to my wife, how God sees me, and how I failed myself. I feel ashamed and burdened again.

As I masturbate I am excited, no longer worried about life or conflicts. Feel euphoric and free.

As I masturbate to a video about _____, I am getting distracted from my worries, escaping the anxiety of the event and it's feelings. I hunt and stimulate myself to keep the escape until I find the right video for escape.

Finding Relief

Feeling Remorse

Taking Action

Promises to Reform

Deciding on Action

Relaxation

Action Choices

Triggering Event

Negative Feelings

Negative Thinking

Constant accusations of failure, confrontation, and suggestions that I am failing.

My efforts are never enough, and go unrecognized. This isn't fair. What's the used anymore.

I feel rejected, unfairly treated and lonely. Anxious and alone. Frustrated and hopeless.

I can escape to porn, this won't hurt and I deserve it. I will feel better. This will be the last time.

Once my wife goes to bed, I will be able to watch some videos. It will be okay because it won't hurt anyone and I can hide it. I'll hunt for the right video and things will be okay.

help of that second pair of eyes, look to see if there are any missing pieces or new revelations to consider. Once you are *both* satisfied with the final version, you can move on to relapse prevention.

Setting Up for Success

Relapse Prevention

Relapse prevention is an identified *and written* plan which identifies opportunities to choose better when confronted with negative triggers, thoughts, and feelings. To be effective, your plan must be written, and address all the steps that precede the taking of action in box 6. From box 6 on you would be in full relapse, so the plan for that half of the cycle will be addressed later in the relapse *recovery* plan.

You are constructing an *action plan* that will divert you from your now identified cycle for boxes 1-5. Be specific, because this plan is what you will be sharing with your wife, accountability partners, group, or others depending on who you have in your life to account to.

Your final plan should follow the same flow as your addiction cycle, from negative event to action. Only, in this case, you will challenge each step along the way. When a negative event happens, challenge the automatic negative thought by having a positive reframe already in hand and well-practiced. For example, if your boss fails to see your contribution to an outcome, instead of telling yourself that you deserve better and that you will sooth yourself with porn, say, "I know I did well, and that is what's important because my reward is in my self-appraisal, not his."

Each box around the circle needs alternatives that speak directly to your *habitual* responses. If, for instance, you habitually ruminate on negative thoughts, you need to have some thought reframes ready to counteract those negative ruminations. Techniques such as *radical acceptance* can help pull you out of such negative thinking. This technique, from Dialectical Behavior Therapy helps reduce overwhelming stress by practicing tolerance of distress, to prevent the event from morphing into suffering. This is done by acknowledging the facts and recognizing that denial or rumination of those facts will not change them. This helps one to accept the things that cannot be changed, not as a victim, but as a wise person. Rumination leads to thoughts of victimization and self-pity. Radical acceptance allows for something to be unpleasant without assigning unfairness, recognizing that many things in life are outside of an individual's control, and that coping is possible.

If it is a negative feeling that results from events that takes you down the addiction path, have a challenge to those typical feelings, such as using *emotional intelligence* techniques to *observe* the feelings, *identify* where they come from, and remember that *feelings are transient*, but *actions can be permanent*. Many people make short term decisions based on negative feelings which create long term consequences they regret. Keep that in mind. Use alternate thoughts and choices to challenge the urgency of any negative feelings. For choices, remember that the practiced drop-down menu of choices in your mind are based on prior established feelings. These are linked to those things you have grown to believe will satisfy or eliminate the potency of those feelings. Change the list of options and you will be less likely to relapse fully into your addiction cycle.

Memorialize your plan. To create your relapse prevention plan, add a fourth column to your original behavior chain table. Label this column Relapse Prevention Plan. In each cell to the right of column three, refer to your charted cycle, and consider an alternative, what you *might* have done, thought, or felt differently, if you only knew what you know now. Column 4 will contain those alternate behaviors, revised thoughts, or better solutions to your feelings based on the following:

- What were/are the *consequences* of this behavior? Be specific.
- How did other people *react* immediately and later?
- How did you *feel* immediately following the behavior? Later?
- What *effect* did the behavior have on you and your environment?

1. *Describe in detail different solutions to the problem.* Here you will explore alternatives and escape routes. List better coping strategies, hints, and alternate choices. Follow the prompts below to help develop your column four.
2. *Go back to the chain of your behaviors following the prompting event.* Circle each point or link indicating that if you had done something different, you would have avoided the problem behavior.
3. *Was there another thought, feeling, or action that could have occurred?* Could someone else have thought, felt, or acted differently at that point? If so, explain how that specific thought, feeling, or action came to be.
4. *What could you have done differently* at each link in the chain of events to avoid the problem behavior? What

coping behaviors or skillful behaviors could you have used?

5. *Describe in detail* a prevention strategy for how you could have kept the chain from starting by reducing your vulnerability in that moment or at that step in the chain.

6. *Describe what you are going to do* to repair important or significant consequences of the problem behavior.

Once you have completed this plan, review it with your coach, accountability partner, or counselor. You want to get feedback to be sure that it is doable, complete, and something you can and will commit to. When it is finalized, give copies to your coach and any accountability partners. Keep two copies, one for you and one to share with your spouse when the time comes. You will use this plan to hold yourself accountable and they will use it with you to do the same for you.

Relapse Recovery Planning

Having come this far, the rest should be easy! You now know why you have developed the addiction(s) that plagued you. You have also arrested the behavior and are clean from porn. The goal here is to *never relapse*. But failing to plan for a relapse is a fatal flaw in many addiction recovery processes. You do not need to relapse, and there is a high probability that you will not. But failing to plan is planning to fail. In many programs, relapse is expected as a normal event, and so it is not seen as a major barrier to sobriety. This is why 12 step and other programs define the recovery process as a verb, being in recovery, for the rest of your life. We do not want to go to validate that extreme. However, we do accept that some people may relapse, and for that we must have a recovery plan;

one that is effective at *redeeming* post-relapse and is also a *deterrent* to relapses in the first place.

First, are you lapsing or relapsing? Remember, we defined lapses and relapses differently in an early section. A lapse is when you are tempted, considering, or thinking about using porn. A relapse is *anything* beyond that. Relapse begins when Box 5 activities are pointed towards acting out. If Box 5 is not healthy, you **will** proceed to Box 6 and be in full relapse. Box 6 is taking any action that is engaging in the actual addictive behavior. For a smoker, it could be walking into a minimart intending to buy cigarettes, or an alcoholic getting into his car to drive to the liquor store, or a porn addict arranging his schedule so that later in the day he can have the privacy or opportunity to view porn or masturbate. When lapsing, the actual relapse can begin long before you even turn on your device. Do not forget that.

Your relapse recovery plan *must include* a confession to your accountability partner(s) that you *are relapsing*. In theory, you would have told them that you were lapsing if that urge was getting strong *prior* to Box 5 activities. Regardless, you must tell them as quickly as possible so that you can prevent the actual use of porn or the collapse of your whole plan.

To accomplish this last part of your plan, you will continue column four, and complete the remaining boxes 6-9 in your cycle. These steps are to be used when you have relapsed (taken action to use or cheat). They are also helpful to review when you are still in the lapse stage because they remind you of what is coming if you relapse; the cost of relapsing should be high so that it deters you from passing Box 5.

For each box beginning with Box 6, assume that you have repeated your identified cycle in the here and now. Consider all the collateral damage that will occur once discovered or confessed, even if you have not yet been discovered. Think about how you will confess to your partners and your spouse, what it would feel like, the shame that will activate, all the realities of your addictive cycle coming back to life.

Draft a response to Boxes 6-9 that describes what you WILL DO NOW to make amends, repair damages, stop future actions, and be accountable. This includes telling your spouse, your accountability partner(s), coach, counselor, pastor, etc. Be brutal with yourself, because at this point you are in danger of staying addicted for life. Make a pledge to yourself that you will also be sharing with them, to hold yourself accountable to the plan.

Your Finalized Relapse Prevention and Recovery Plan

This "plan" is a generic example of what someone might write for their plan. Yours should be specific to *your* cycle so that you, your spouse, and your accountability partner(s) can understand it and help you track your place and progress easily.

Example Relapse Prevention/Recovery Plan

My Behavior Cycle	My Relapse Prevention Plan	My Relapse Recovery Plan
Event(s) that commonly Trigger my cycle	Events do not necessarily need to imply anything about me. I can let them go or I can check my assumptions.	*When I feel triggered, and I fail to reframe the event in a productive way, I will confess to others that I am reacting and why it's a problem.*
The negative Thoughts behind my cycle	My thoughts are mine to control. I do not need to assume and react negatively, especially to things outside my control.	*When my thoughts become negative after an event, I will write out a "thought dispute" or thought challenge and check where I am going wrong, then take responsibility for my thinking errors, or let go of things that are out of my control.*

194 The Renewed Mind

The Feelings that come up because of my thoughts	I chose to feel the way I feel because I am not keeping my thoughts well. I will stop and think about what I am feeling, why it was triggered, and then work to let it go by.	*When I fail to keep my emotions rational and balanced, I will take responsibility and apologize, confess, or repair the damage I have done in reacting towards others or myself.*
My internal Reaction to my feelings (fight/flight/freeze)	When I feel overwhelmed, I know I will want to react with action. So, I will choose my reactions from a health list of options I have pre-determined, not allowing myself to react in habit or rashly.	*When I choose to react with a fight or flight, and that choice leads me to relapse, I will acknowledge to my spouse & accountability partner my responsibility, and to do what I can to correct any damage or hurt I caused, and to rehearse with them a better alternative so next time will be*

		less likely to happen.
How I Set UP my behavior to deal with my reaction	I will not allow myself to get closer to the opportunity to relapse by not accessing my phone/devices when triggered to anger or unhealthy coping. I will place blocks on my devices or give them to my accountability partner or tell my spouse I am in trouble and need help.	*With excruciating detail, I will confess how I set up the opportunity to relapse or how I took advantage of opportunities, worked around my blocks, or deceived my accountability partners/spouse so I could act out.*
The Actions I tend to use to reduce my reactive response to thoughts and feelings	I will not use selfish actions to gratify my momentary desire to self-sooth. I will find my relief in my real relationships with God, myself, and my family/friends.	*If I do act out, I will immediately tell all those to whom I am accountable, explain in detail what, how, why, and when I acted out, and take responsibility for my actions. This*

	Being alone in my self-abuse is not allowed.	*may cost me deeply, but I will keep my word to be transparent.*
How I experience Relief once I act out	I know I can't truly get anything but more pain from acting on my addictions. I will choose to follow a higher mission in my life and find my satisfaction in my vision of a better me.	*If I self-molest to get my relief, I will immediately invite my accountability partners and spouse to take this problem to God in confession, and make a true and transparent repentance, out loud, and in their presence.*
The Remorse I feel after acting out	I know that no amount of shame and guilt will stop me from acting out in the future but will actually make it more likely. I will not use my guilt or shame tendencies to justify my future likelihood	*If I find myself in a place of self-pity, I will challenge myself by making deeper confessions to those I am letting down, and not ask them for forgiveness or pity, but ask them to hold me*

	of relapse. No excuses permitted.	*strongly accountable for my willful choices.*
How I make False Promises to relieve my remorse. How does my false promise Set Up my future?	I know that a false promise to reform myself is self-manipulation, and if I make false promises to my spouse or accountability partners, I am practicing deceit and manipulation. I will be truthful even if it means being exposed.	*If I find myself making false promises to self or to others, I will confess this BEFORE I am challenged and immediately take the accountability consequences without defense.*

Review these plans with your coach or counselor for feedback. Once you've agreed that they are complete, share them with your accountability partners and your spouse. If you relapse, your accountability partners will be expecting you to follow through on your plan. They should challenge you on which parts of the plan were skipped by you or were ineffective so that you can plug those holes for the future. The anticipation of this accountability interaction, along with the other built-in consequences will keep you mindful of how important it is to not ever get back into relapse.

Be sure to build in strong consequences if you can, to keep you mindful of how important it is to not ever get back into relapse. Once you have reviewed all the plans with those who will hold you accountable, gather them together with your cycle and supporting materials, plus your victim impact statement, your safety plan, and any other assignments. *Do not* include your chain or your deep dive. These should be destroyed once you are done.

Once you have reviewed the plans, gather your VIS, your Safety Plan, your Addiction Cycle, and your Relapse Prevention/Recovery plan together. You will be using these materials for final documentation and presentation to your spouse at whatever level she can handle. Sometimes, too much at one time will overwhelm a spouse who is still suffering from the trauma of betrayal, so get advice and guidance from your coach on what should be shared fully, and what might need to be shared slowly.

Eventually, you and she will want to review it all so the final walls of secrecy and not knowing can fall away. Most of you working with one of my coaches or with me will have presented each of these various exercises to your spouse when they are completed. But for those working alone, you may not have been able to, or have excused yourself from that requirement. If this is so, your task will be harder because giving it all to her at once is likely to create quite a reaction. And it will likely force you back to do some revisions since each part sets up the next. Transparency and effective future success demand that your spouse and your accountability partner(s) need to know and comprehend these process lessons and plans if they are to effectively hold you accountable to your own worst tendencies with your chosen strategies.

Do not include your behavior chain or your deep dive in the materials you provide to your spouse. These can be destroyed, once you are positive that you are completely done (including the presentations to your spouse), since they have no further purpose or value to you. These should NOT be included in your disclosure to your spouse. Not because it's keeping secrets, but because they have a high likelihood of traumatizing or triggering your wife unnecessarily. These are unnecessary because this is your childhood history and your worst moments in life. They happened and cannot be undone. She will not benefit from seeing them, and you both may suffer from revealing anything that is too personal from childhood that she does not truly need to know. Remember, you cannot un-ring a bell, and some things cannot be unsaid or easily forgotten. The last thing we want to do is establish a fear of judgment and shame in you, or any persistent fears in your wife. Sometimes history must be deleted for the right reasons.

Many wives question why I insist that you remove the behavior chain and deep dive, feeling threatened because it seems to them it is *keeping secrets* from them. But I truly urge you not to keep or include these two parts of your work. Not because I like to keep secrets, but because they have a high likelihood of traumatizing or triggering your wife. She will not benefit from seeing them, and you will suffer from revealing anything that is too personal from childhood that she does not truly need to know. Shame is YOUR enemy, not hers, and something that, as a woman, she cannot comprehend in the same way a man sees it. Having your childhood burned into your spouse's memory, which will become connected to your recent acts of betrayal, will only cause you and her future problems. Remember, you cannot unring a bell, and some things cannot be unsaid or easily forgotten. The last thing we want to do is establish a *fear of judgment and shame* in you, or any persistent fears in your wife. Sometimes history must be deleted for the right reasons. These examples have no further purpose. The past, while informative for your recovery and growth, should no longer be held onto.

Now that you have examined your life and how addiction took over your reward-response systems, unlocked the steps that bound you to addiction, and developed a plan to recover and prevail, it is time to move to the most crucial step in your life-long change. It is time to recover the Man of Valor you were called to be.

The Man of Valor

Many of the men I work with are military in their vocation. Their experiences are often vastly different from my civilian upbringing. They are an inexhaustible source of new learning for me in ways that never cease to amaze. In a recent conversation with an active-duty client, I was describing an event from my past. I do not recall why I shared this piece of personal history, but I am sure it was useful to his session, or I would not have disclosed. It was his reaction that impacted me, however.

I was telling him about my experience learning to drive when I was fifteen. Our school had a driver's training program, in which three kids learned to drive with an instructor over the course of about eight weeks. I recall the first week vividly, with myself, a guy named Mike (whose last name I do not recall), and a girl named Laura whose last name I vividly to this day (but will leave it out). I remember exactly what she looked like as if she were sitting next to me right now. And I know her vice as clearly as my best friend's. Not for the reasons most young men vividly recall a high school girl. It was because I thought she was going to kill us all, many times over.

Our first day out in the little car with our instructor, we all took turns at the wheel for the first time on a street with real cars. Mike had claimed some driving experience on his grandpa's farm, so he went first. Then it was my turn. Finally, going last because she was scared was Laura. Mr. Willis was sure she would do fine, so we did not really think much about it. Mike and I in the back seat, now the experts for having driven for over ten minutes each, offered our reassurances too.

As we started down the two-lane road along the outskirts of our small town, we were all happy and feeling potent as teens tend to do, until a truck came into view traveling the opposite direction. The road was wide, and there was a nice yellow line down the middle. The cars in the late seventies for drivers training were little Japanese imports, so we occupied little space in our own lane. The truck coming in the other direction was also within his own lane. There was no cause for concern.

At first no one thought much about it. That is, until we noticed that Laura was starting to drift to the left, moving slowly but steadily towards the center of the road. Mike, being on the driver's side, was first to notice, and pointed it out to all of us. Mr. Willis was not worried. He told us to relax. But, as the truck got closer to us, Laura got closer to the line. We were getting scared. With plenty of time to spare, Mr. Willis reached over and steered the car back to its proper place in the lane. He never said a word.

Over the next two weeks, this happened repeatedly, only there was more traffic as we were beginning to use the main roads, and then there was the freeway. Mike and I were terrified. The near-death encounters seemed to never end. Mr. Willis kept turning the wheel back, or coaxing Laura to do so until finally she stopped this drifting toward certain death. Eventually we all passed our course, and our license exams, and I never thought much about it other than to have occasional dreams about it even now.

I sometimes use stories like this to make a point with clients. In this case, the client responded very enthusiastically, "target fixation!" he burst out. "I know what that is." It was his turn to introduce me to something new. He informed me from his motorcycle training that the term *target fixation* [an attentional phenomenon] described the way people become focused on an observed object that they inadvertently steer in the direction of their gaze, which often causes a collision or the risk of colliding. He knew it also was a problem for fighter pilots.

The idea resonated with me because I have seen a similar phenomenon in the men I treat for porn and cyber-sexual or gaming addictions. Where their attention is, so go they. Target fixation seems to apply to building or extinguishing habits as well. Using that idea, I have started to instill this thought into my men's recovery work, and the results have been promising. Perhaps it is a form of target fixation that makes the last part of this recovery process so powerful. Let us get on with the final stage of the Covenant Man process, restoring the Man of Valor.

The Mighty Man of Valor on a Mission of Valor

The term *Man of Valor* may be overused, but I picked it for my treatise on porn recovery for its tremendous potential to transform lives beyond mere recovery from cyber-addictions. In the Old Testament, we read about King David and his Mighty Men (2nd Samuel), and Gideon who was declared a Man of Valor by the Lord (Judges 6:12). The concept of being a man of valor comes up over thirty times in the Old Testament. God has an expectation of men, and *valor* identifies those men who fit that calling.

The Mighty Man of Valor traits are visible in King David's three chieftains, in their actions: Leadership with **Might** (potency, capacity, effectiveness), with **Valor** (courage, fortitude, determination, honor), and with **Devotion** (attachment, zeal, regard, esteem, fidelity).

The First Chieftain-Leadership through Might, leading with *courage* and *example. He* slew eight hundred people with a sword. He was known for leadership, by placing himself in the front of the action. Valorous leaders lead with examples. Mighty leaders are willing to pay the cost that they ask of others.

The Second Chieftain-Demonstration of Valor, the next *stood his ground.* All the rest of the Israelites ran, while he alone stood to fight the enemy. Standing alone is hard, even disastrous. But when conviction is true, standing is the only option. To be truly valorous, you must be willing to take a stand.

The Third Chieftain-Devotion to Mission, was *steadfast* and *devoted* in his duty alone and overwhelmed. But he stayed true, keeping the interests of God and his people ahead of his own self-interest, and waited on God to win the day. To be steadfast, hold the ground and wait on God.

The Mighty Man of Valor in Action

Relationship with (and duty to) God

- A mighty man of valor puts God first.
- A mighty man of valor knows his purpose and keeps his mission at the forefront of his thoughts.
- A mighty man of valor is one who relies on God while realizing he cannot fulfill his mission alone.
- A mighty man of valor takes risks when God instructs him forward, despite fear or doubt.

Relationship with (and duty to) Self

- A mighty man of valor always takes care of his responsibilities.
- A mighty man of valor does not settle for talk, he walks the walk openly.
- A mighty man of valor goes through the eye of the storm with confidence.
- A mighty man of valor engages problems with action.

Relationship with (and duty to) his Wife

- A mighty man of valor does not make his love conditional.
- A mighty man of valor loves his wife Christ loved the Church, willing and ready to lay down his own life, selfish desires, even needs if necessary, so that he can lift up his wife.

- A mighty man of valor lives love according to 1 Corinthians 13.

Relationship with (and duty to) his Family

- A mighty man of valor places his family ahead of himself. He knows that his mission is to support them and their future.
- A mighty man of valor never tears his family down, he strives to lift them up.

Relationship with (and duty to) Others in his life and circle.

- A mighty man of valor has compassion for others, seeking to help, not to harm.
- A mighty man of valor demonstrates the love of God to everyone by being obedient to scripture, showing love even his enemies.

Your Circles of Action

"...you will receive power when the Holy Spirit has come upon you; and you shall be My witnesses both in Jerusalem, and in all Judea and Samaria, and even to the remotest part of the earth."
Acts 1:8

A Mighty Man of Valor is on a mission. The personal or individual application of Acts 1:8 helps guide and instruct people on the nature of personal mission. Jerusalem was the center of the world, and the disciples began there. They extended their ministry outward, to reach Judea and Samaria, and eventually, they brought the mission to the entire world. Likewise, individuals have their own circles of action.

Self, Spouse, Family, and The World. As an individual, you affect your home most directly. Home can be the circle of influence you have over your literal home and family, as well as your closest friends and companions. Extending from that you find your *Judea and Samaria* in your work environment, associations, community, and the world.

A Man of Valor is mission driven and knows that his actions influence the circles that surround him. His actions extend telically from his center and like ripples on a pond, have a purposeful destination or outcome.

This book has substantially replicated my ongoing *Covenant Men's* group process for overcoming cybersexual and arousal addictions. Along the way, you have simultaneously learned the tenets of valorous living as a *Man of Valor*. This was intentional. If you are to defeat any strongholds in your life you must have a greater sense of mission and self than the addictions and habits that ensnare you. Over the years, habits have formed from behaviors that originated in your childhood and youth. Those habits have been inculcated into your life so firmly that you are oblivious to their level of control over everyday living. We would call this an *insurgency*; an internal rebellion against the righteous authority of your God given purpose for life.

An insurgency requires a strong counteraction to safeguard your identity and personal autonomy in life. In Covenant Men, we use warfare as the metaphorical model to help men fight the insurgency. Men understand the need for war. Men accept war when those people and values they hold dear are at stake.

In the case of addictions, your entire wellbeing, and that of your primary relationships, are at direct risk. It is time for war. It is time for The Man of Valor to step up into action.

A Mission of Valor

Alice was lost. Alice was scared. Alice was confused.

Alice came to a fork in the road.

'Which road do I take?' she asked.

'Where do you want to go?' responded the Cheshire Cat.

'I don't know,' Alice answered.

'Then,' said the Cat, 'It doesn't matter.' [15]

Not knowing where you want to go, or what you want from yourself seems to be a common state of mind in today's America. This not knowing leaves a massive hole in your self-identity. Compulsive behaviors, decisions in the moment, and addictions each offer to fill this hole—at least for the moment. Life lived in the present only.

Living in a State of "I Don't Know" (the Alice in Wonderland paradox).

When you are feeling like Alice did, lost without knowing what you want for your life will simply spin you into the chaos of whatever the moment offers. The result is reactive emotions, conflict, confusion, depression, loneliness, hopelessness, and poor decision making. What a great recipe for disaster! Addiction eagerly wants to find you and solve all of this with its false promise of satisfaction in the face of pain and despair.

Now try to imagine, just for a moment, that you could use the same drive for relief, the very source of power that the addiction latches on to and *turn it back on itself*. What would it be like if you could simply know before you arrive at a crossroad which way will take you to the best possible outcome? Addiction would lose all power to tempt you since you would no longer be desperate, lost, or vulnerable to making poor decisions.

With some minor readjustments in your mental perception into the realities of life, you can do just that. Defeating compulsive decision making is really that simple but it does require some planning.

How Compulsion Works

Oscar Wilde once said that he *"could resist everything but temptation."*

The power of compulsion towards sin or towards righteousness is found in your brain's pursuit of the neurotransmitter dopamine, that feel-good brain chemical that rewards behavior.

The purpose of dopamine is to *train the brain* to seek out choices that bring success, and to avoid pain. In simple terms, the release of dopamine by your brain's pleasure center floods you with that euphoric feeling we perceive as pleasantness, content, joy, relief, and other warn fuzzy feelings. Experiencing a dopamine release, or in some cases a dopamine RUSH declares our choice was effective.

Dopamine is a powerful motivator! But, the absence of dopamine does not punish us, it just does not trigger these good feelings. The opposite effect of dopamine comes when we are at risk of not achieving whatever it is that we associate with a dopamine reward. When you are on target for that dopamine reward, anything that deters you or stops you is seen as a barrier to our goal of getting to the feel-good outcome.

This trigger is anxiety and activates your arousal system to defense. **Anxiety is also a powerful motivator.** We all naturally strive to avoid anxiety.

The Wild Ride of Addiction

Dopamine does not differentiate between moral or ethical, good, or bad. It is not selective, it is *reactive*. Its only purpose is to provide a *strong positive reinforcement*, not a moral or socially appropriate one. When combined with its opposite motivational force, *anxiety*, the mind becomes conditioned to repeat the success of acquiring dopamine, and to avoid the anxiety of failure. The brain approves of this successful goal achievement by providing a dopamine surge.

It works like this, first formulate a target, which we call a goal. A simple goal might be "I'm hungry." You then plot a path towards food. That path is a series of patterned actions which you have *learned* will result in food, the completion of which will in turn satisfy your goal. Your patterned actions are specifically goal-oriented and make decision making easy. Each decision, each action moves you closer to fulfilment. Each time you get closer, dopamine rewards you with another spike, reinforcing your belief that you are doing the right thing. Through the rewarding release of dopamine, you experience positive emotions.

Anything that interferes with your chosen path toward your goal produces a *stress response,* anxiety, which is a negative emotional experience. This causes you to stop and figure it out what threat or barrier to your reward is present, and then how to reverse or change your direction. This anxiety response causes you to avoid pain or fear in the natural but works the same for all reward-driven goal pursuits, addictions in particular. In this example, when you achieve the goal and get the food, dopamine rewards you and confirms your action plan is correct. Therefore, if you find relief every day by going through a McDonalds drive through, you will quickly become convinced this is the correct action to take. Here is where habits are born and reinforced.

Now, let us imagine you are on your way to McDonald's just like usual when suddenly another car hits yours. Injured and trapped in your car, you find yourself waiting for the jaws-of-life to get you free and an ambulance to take you to a hospital. Understandably, your earlier goal of getting a Big Mac is no longer important. The larger goal of survival and pain relief dismisses the lesser hunger goal. The new goal is based on how you *now perceive* reality. Reality has not changed. You have always needed to survive and be pain free. It is just that now the threat to your survival is more than just finding food. The new goal of *surviving and being pain free* is a much bigger goal than your previous goal of *stop feeling hungry*.

Habits are patterns designed to arrive at a goal *perceived* to be important. Some are good, some not so much. But they are simply patterns **chosen** because the brain has accepted and reinforced them as they tend to successfully arrive at that dopamine release. Habits compete for priority based on the perceived needs of the moment. In that moment, all beliefs about the choice of behaviors become reinforced and justified.

Addiction is more than a simple habit. Addiction is a destructive habit. It has trained the brain to perceive the cause of the addiction as the *biggest need in general,* not just the moment. Addiction is a primary survival focus, overriding your true needs for survival. Addiction creates a condition of *an independent personality*, based on a whole new identity. That personality is always going to be a liar, a cheat, and completely selfish. It is a destructive form of narcissism. And it is a complete façade that overwhelms the true self. Addicts are not human beings; they are human doings—doing whatever is necessary to get to the end goal is all that matters to the addict.

When someone is trying to connect with you to stop your addictive behavior, they typically are met by the personality of the addiction, not the authentic you. Naturally, a conflict ensues because the addiction only wants to attain the goal of dopamine release, and the interfering person is now a perceived enemy threatening the dopamine supply. Stress creates an anxiety response (stops you in your tracks to figure it out how to remove the obstacle, mostly by arguing, blame shifting, gaslighting, etc.) or a pain/fear response, turns you away to find a less resistant path (deception, lying, etc.) to fulfil your addictive goal.

Choosing your Path.

Dopamine does not choose, it simply responds. Choice is the product of a higher level of brain functioning (and a different neurotransmitter release). Choice overrides the hypothalamic control of the moment and predetermines what success looks like. This guides the dopamine release to reinforce what you chose, not what simply feels good in the moment. If you want victory over addiction and its compulsive behaviors, you must learn to use the primary motivators of reward and stress to your advantage—towards a purpose bigger than just living in the moment. If you do this one basic thing, above all other things, you will effectively turn the tide against rewarding bad choices and begin to experience automatic thinking that rewards good choices.

Not Simply Willpower

When I was a high school sophomore, my social studies teacher made us listen to a recording of *The Odyssey* by Homer. He tried to show us the tenacity of Odysseus to fulfil his quest, despite the temptations and obstacles that had to face to get back home. I must confess, I missed the deeper meanings of the entire story at sixteen. Only the adventures were interesting: The Cyclops, the Trojan Horse, and especially the story of the Siren's song. Often, the story of Odysseus versus the Sirens' song is used to demonstrate one's ability to resolve or resist temptation—we call it self-determination or will power. But is it really?

My answer is a resounding *no!* Odysseus did not use willpower to resist the Sirens call. He *planned* against the irresistible force that would overpower his self-control in the moment. In preparation, he had himself tied to the mast of his ship so that despite the Siren's call, he had no choice but to sail by. This is not willpower; it is motivation to a higher goal established *before* the temptation has a chance to fill in the gaps of desire. I now understand more of Odysseus's quest than I did as a teen. Perseverance to a higher goal, in Odysseus' case, to prove his identity and allow him to retake his throne, clearly shows how a strong motivation overcomes otherwise insurmountable goals. This is why I call our men's support group the Overcomer's Group.

To control dopamine so that it will motivate you *in the right way*, you must first establish an objective *bigger than porn* or the other habits that are competing for the easiest or accustomed dopamine reward. Like Odysseus, a bigger goal must prevail to resist the Siren's call. In his case it was his *life's mission and vision*, represented by his quest. He had to return home to his rightful place, recover his family, and take back his throne. Does this sound familiar to you? It should. Your quest in life is the same: reclaim your rightful place, recover the sanctity and health of your marriage and family, and take back your throne as the leader in your household. Addictions take all that away from you. It is time to take them back!

Here is How it Works:

Creating a self that is *bigger than* the addicted self allows the person affected by addiction to retake their rightful throne, be reunited with their true family, and resume a healthy life. This can only happen when the dopamine response system *restructures* in favor of the true self versus the addiction. A *healthy* pursuit of dopamine activates dramatic personal change—change that becomes just as automatic as it was with addiction, but for a better outcome, an authentic self.

Beginning with the smallest of change, an intentional focus towards a new target goal can compound with successes day by day. This leads to a mindful assessment of what will be, instead of living for what currently has captured the dopamine response system. This is a new perception of reality, and one totally controlled by your choice of action, in *advance* of the Siren song.

Creative tension is motivation that drives you on the path to achieving a greater outcome. It's the positive side of anxiety, driven by the difference between what you are currently achieving in life, and what you envision you can achieve. Like cognitive dissonance, it is a strong motivator for change. You instinctively seek emotional assurance through positive reward, which triggers dopamine. If this reward is bigger than your current addictive goal, your mind will steer around or retreat from the negative emotion of stress and anxiety of using porn because porn is now blocking your access to the bigger goal.

It starts with small movements forward but becomes more powerful because the *anticipation* of attaining the new target goal causes dopamine to release as each step brings you closer to the end goal, in the same way porn built up your dopamine reward in the early stages of your addiction. The compounding effect of anticipation and reward reinforces this motivational drive, replacing the addiction with self-actualizing success. Over time the false promise of addiction becomes evident in full. Only then will true freedom and joy prevail.

How Do I Establish That Bigger Than Porn Goal?

Let's go back to Alice and the Cheshire Cat. Choosing a direction will matter only when you know where you want to go. The Word of God tells:

> "Where there is no vision, the people perish… but he that keeps the law is happy." *Proverbs 29:18*

"My people are destroyed for lack of knowledge; because they reject knowledge, I will also reject them, they will not be a priest to me: because the forgot the law of thy God, I will also forget their children." *Hosea 4:6,*

What ties these two scriptures together is *vision*. Vision is simply *knowledge*. Knowing who you are in Christ is the only way to be connected to God, be the priest in your family, and bless your children. Vision is knowing the scripture well enough to know you were *intended* to be fulfilled in Christ. Accurately defining yourself is the only way to beat addictive behaviors and stupid momentary choices. A man of God is a man of virtue. But at least in modern western culture, not very many lessons are taught to boys about what it is to be a man, especially a virtuous man.

To overcome and extinguish a destructive addiction pattern, you must first establish a true vision of self as an outcome. This challenges the addiction's irrational understanding of reality. Challenging the tenets of addiction erases the faulty convictions that you are who you are only because of where you came from, what you have done, or even what you have continued to do.

Reality is contained in *Truth* and is discoverable. Yet most people just accept their current perception of reality based on the lies developed through the experiences of their addiction. They simply accept that they are who the addiction has made them to be. But Truth is greater than that fiction. Truth comes from God, truth is immutable, and truth can be known. Once you know the Truth about yourself, you will begin to experience a dissonance between the life of addiction and the life that should and could be. A life that is based on your true self. We will call this revealed truth *perspective.*

Once you establish Truth, the perspective between the two lives (creative tension) can become a powerful motivator for change. John Maxwell[16] said that *people must learn enough to want to change* before they will willingly make the effort to change. What and who you are in Truth is much bigger than anything else this world has to offer you, because it reflects how God has defined your purposed. This is the only goal that is big enough to do the job of permanently blotting out your addictions. To truly change perspectives, you must learn to see correctly.

To Discover and Become That True Self:

1. **Search scripture** for the definitions of manhood, husbandry, and fatherhood.
   - From those scriptures, define what you MUST look and act like to conform to that definition of self.
   - Create a vision of self. **Write it down**, as if it were already a fact, already fulfilled. Frame it as a statement as if God were telling it to others. Declaring in heaven what kind of man you are. Be concise but be complete.
2. **Tell yourself**, your wife, and your kids who you are (in the process of is okay but use "as if it's already true" language). "God called me to be a man of honor and integrity, a father that puts his children ahead of his own needs, a husband who loved his wife as much, even more, than he loves his own life, a servant who places people in high regard simply because they are children of God...." Get the idea?
3. Determine the path to fulfillment.
   - What are you doing that brings you closer (dopamine reward for doing these)?

- What should you be doing better or start doing (anticipatory dopamine reward)?
- What are you doing that blocks you (stress anxiety negative motivator)?

4. **Become the goal**: Know yourself and begin to speak that self-understanding into being so that it becomes real in your mind, as well as to your soul. Your body will follow because it is subject to you.
   - Colossians 2:10 You are made complete in Christ.
   - Matthew 6:22 "Your eyes are windows into your body. If you open your eyes wide in wonder and belief, your body fills up with light."
   - Matthew 12:35, "A good man out of the good treasure of his heart brings forth good things, and an evil man out of the evil treasure brings forth evil things."

Having a Vison for Life

In business school I was taught that success can only come once a vision has been established. The same holds true for our personal lives. From birth begins a process of knowing self and knowing how we fit into the world. However, to succeed to the maximum level of our ability, you must establish a healthy and mighty self-vision.

Relationships are defined and driven by your success in overcoming any struggles you have with relating, in a healthy way, to your own self. Growing up is all about discovering who you are and learning to live in a healthy relationship with *the self*. All other relationships extend from your personal journey of self and the (hopefully healthy) vision of self you create and hold. To do this fully, you must first develop a sense of relationship *with and in* God, who is much bigger than you and your *self*, and who is also the very definition of love and relationship. God demonstrates perfect relationship with His own *self* in the three persons of His self—Father, Jesus, Holy Spirit.

To find one's True self six levels of understanding must be developed. To be fully realized, they need to be in a progressive order of development.

1. **Understand the nature of God in relationship** to His own self by understanding how He relates to Himself. He is expressed in three natures, God the father (the mind and power), God in the Holy Spirit, which is his nature being expressed, and as the Word, which became flesh as Jesus, who is the personality of God incarnate. He relates to Himself as *Us* in some scriptures and He exists in a united harmony with His separate expressions of self. This models family and relationship to us in function.

2. **Understand how God relates to you personally,** and how you relate back to Him. This relationship between God and Himself sets the foundation for all other relationships in life. God wants to relate to you. He created you to love, and be loved, Him for you, and you for Him.

3. **Understand you relate to your own self.** This relating to self allows us to reconcile the parts of our

own being—the primary expressions of self: Spiritual self (our value, worth, or existential being), Personal self (the emotional self that feels) and the Mindful self (cognitive thought and ability to know the self and others). Just as God is united in His various natures, so we must be.

4. **Understand how you relate to your spouse in partnership**, joining two selves into one life mission. Marriage is not losing self, it is joining in a mission that allows for the full expression of self *between* to human beings, much as the Church as the Bride of Christ allows God and Man to join in full expression one to the other.

5. **Understand how you relate to your children/family**, as an expression of your marriage, your own self, and with God.

6. **Understand how you relate to the rest of the world** as an expression of self and your union with God, self, and family.

"Getting leadership right begins with leading yourself well." Andy Stanley

Character from Virtue

Most Christians are familiar with C.S. Lewis and his works. One of my favorites has always been the Chronicles of Narnia. I was once privileged to speak with Professor Mark Pike from Leeds University in England, when he visited my university, to present on **Narnian Virtues: A Character Education Curriculum**[17] which he and his colleagues developed for use in middle school in England.

As I listened, I was struck with understanding why these classic children's books by Lewis were so powerful. As Pike explained, Lewis had built into his series the **universal virtues** that establish **character.** These virtues are not simply good, they are Godly. Twelve Narnian Virtues were identified and grouped by Pike and his colleagues into six themes: **wisdom, love, integrity, self-control, fortitude,** and **justice.** They defined virtues as **"good moral habits;** *good character consists of these good habits. If a person is 'of good character,' then he or she will have developed a range of virtues (good habits)."* This should remind you of the process of principles we learned earlier. Habits produce predictable outcomes.

As you begin to consider your own life's mission expression *to date*, and how it affects your relationship with others, review the Narnian Virtues below and judge for yourself whether you have established each of them well in your life, and how they should be revised, amplified, or included in any new mission or vision going forward.

Check those that must be addressed in your new focused mission going forward that have been underdeveloped in your current life.

☐ **Wisdom**. The habit of exercising good judgement; being able to see what is true and good and choosing the best course of action. Without wisdom, we cannot make good decisions.

☐ **Curiosity.** Part of wisdom is curiosity: the habit of being inquisitive; showing the desire to learn or know something. In general, it is wise to want to learn, but wisdom cautions us not to explore what may be bad for us (such as illegal drugs and the occult or 'bad pictures' such as pornography in magazines or on the Internet). Curiosity is the mark of an active mind, but curiosity about the wrong things can get us in trouble.

☐ **Love.** The habit of acting selflessly for the good of another, without seeking recognition or reward; willingness to sacrifice for the sake of others by putting their well-being ahead of our own; doing good for others by being kind, caring, generous, and loyal. There is no greater love than to lay down one's life for another.

☐ **Forgiveness**. The habit of letting go of anger or resentment toward others who have caused us injury. Forgiving someone who has hurt you is an act of love. Many people find forgiveness difficult when someone has hurt them deeply.

☐ **Gratitude.** The habit of feeling and expressing thanks for benefits received. Gratitude is love expressed. Gratitude leads us to count our blessings.

☐ **Integrity.** The habit of being true to ourselves and truthful with others; standing up for moral principles and following our conscience; not engaging in self-deception, such as telling ourselves that it is OK to do something that, deep down, we know is wrong. If we have integrity, we do not deceive others or ourselves.

☐ **Humility.** The habit of being aware of our strengths and shortcomings; striving to correct our flaws and failures; being free from pride and arrogance. Without humility, pride blinds us to our faults. Humility is an aspect of integrity because it means being honest with self, and others, about our failings. ***"Humility is not thinking less of ourselves but thinking of ourselves less." (C.S. Lewis).***

☐ **Fortitude.** The habit of the doing what is right and necessary in the face of difficulty; the mental and emotional strength, the 'inner toughness,' to endure suffering and overcome adversity; exhibiting qualities such as confidence, courage, perseverance, and resilience when challenging circumstances demand them. They would need fortitude to endure the difficult journey ahead.

☐ **Hard Work.** The habit of working towards a wise goal with energy, commitment, and persistence. You must work hard to meet your goals.

☐ **Courage.** The habit of overcoming fear when facing physical danger or social pressure to do what is wrong. Moral courage—standing up for what is right when it is unpopular to do so—is rarer than bravery in battle.

☐ **Self-control.** The habit of self-restraint; the mastery and moderation of our desires, emotions, impulses, and appetites; resisting temptation; delaying gratification to achieve a higher goal. In the absence of self-control, our desires control us.

☐ **Justice.** The habit of treating everyone with equal respect and fairness; fulfilling our responsibilities; taking responsibility for our actions, admitting when we have done wrong, and making amends; recognizing that no one—including ourselves—is 'above the law.'

I want you to visualize sometime in the future, when life is over, and you have stepped into eternity and heaven. Jesus is there to welcome you. He puts his arm around your shoulder and walks you into the presence of the multitude. He says, *"Welcome to heaven! Let me introduce you to the others."* He walks you up in front of the crowd of all those who have already arrived. Then, He looks at you, smiles, and He looks at them. "I want to introduce you to my beloved brother. Let me tell you about him, his life, and the man he ***truly*** is..." Then He proceeds to describe you vividly and truthfully, revealing all the ways you have lived your life, particularly in how you treated your relationships with others.

Right now, in this moment, as you ponder that visualization of you and Jesus in Heaven, what are you thinking? If this were to happen today, would you be excited or worried about what Jesus had to say about you, your character, and how you impacted those in your life?

1. Ask yourself:
    *   What is it that he would say about me today if He told it all?
    *   Do I feel comfortable with what he would say about me as I am today?
    *   Is there anything that I should change or would like to accomplish that would allow Jesus to testify about me in the way I would hope for?

Begin to make a bullet point list of all the things that you believe that Jesus would say about you *if* you were living your life the way that you believe would please him.

*   What would he say about you and your relationship with God and with him?

- What would he say about your relationship with your own self and your heart?
- What would he say about you and your relationship with your spouse?
- With your family?
- With your work?
- With your friends?
- With the rest of the world at large?

2. **Construct a *brief narrative*** from those bullets that contains the most important parts of what you would *like him to be able to say* about you *as if he was saying it* to everyone in the present moment.

3. **Use *His* words** to create a mission statement for yourself, that is one paragraph, between three to five sentences max. Make it concise. Revise it as needed to meet your view of what you want Jesus to be able to testify about you. Here is an example of what you might write in part.

> *"God called me to be a man of honor and integrity, a father that puts his children ahead of his own needs, a husband who loved his wife as much, even more, than he loves his own life, a servant who places people in high regard simply because they are children of God...."*

4. **Read it back to yourself** *aloud* and with *confidence*. This is who you know you are meant to be because God has said it. When you read it, you must *declare it*.

5. **Visualize yourself** succeeding in being the person of your mission statement. See yourself living out that mission in the here and now. The mind is malleable. It accepts what you order it to accept. Like King David, you need to use declarative self-talk to keep believing what is true.

> *"My soul, wait only upon God and silently submit to Him; for my hope and expectation are from him...He only is my Rock and my Salvation; He is my Defense and my Fortress. I shall*

not be moved...God has spoken once, twice have I heard this; that power belongs to God." Psalm 62:5-6, 11.

To keep you mindful of who you are in vision and mission, make a list of the things you need to add to get there. Make a list of things you must stop doing in order to get there.

6. **Share your mission:** There is power in declaring things to be true. There is increased power in speaking boldly to others. Like prophesying the will and nature of God, speaking forth in Truth establishes it publicly and embeds it in your heart. So, you must learn to share your mission. If you do this well and consistently, you will become known for your vision, which will reinforce you knowing yourself for your vision. Share your mission and vision statement openly and constantly:

    *   With yourself. Read it aloud at least once per day, and silently whenever you see it. Drill it down into your memory. Visualize who you will be, and what God will say about you every time you think of it or see it. Become the man of God you aspire to be every day.

    *   With your wife. Share with her what you will now do to achieve it. She will become your partner in pursuing this new reality.

    *   With your family. Share your mission statement with your kids, parents, and others who are close. They will be your witnesses and best cheerleaders.

    *   Post a copy up where you can see it every day and a copy that others can see as well. Suitable places to post your mission statement is on the mirror where you shave, in your car on the visor or dash, at work on your desk, inside the door of your locker, On the front cover (insider or outside) of any notebooks, computers, or as your screen saver where it will constantly remind you of who you are working to become. You can create a concise mini statement that helps you to be mindful as

well. The one I use sums up my personal vision in a quote which I include on my email signature and as my screen savers, "Don't just count your blessings, be the blessing other people count on!" Having this posted everywhere keeps me mindful of my commitment to God, myself, and others.

7. **Learn more** about how to make your vision stick. In fact, there is a terrific book by Andy Stanly by that very title, *Making Vision Stick*[18]. Here are some notable quotes from Stanley's book:

Seeing a vision become a reality requires more than a single burst of energy or creativity. It requires daily attention. Daily commitment.

Vision does not stick without constant care and attention.

The three primary obstacles to making vision stick are success, failure, and everything in between.

Vision is about what could be and should be, but life is about right this minute.

When it comes to making your vision stick, here is the most important thing to remember: You are responsible.

If the people around us do not know where we are going, it is because we have not made it clear.

For your vision to stick, you may need to clarify or simplify it.

To make vision stick, it needs to be easy to communicate.

Vision needs to be repeated regularly. To make it stick, you need to find ways to build vision casting into the rhythm of your [life].

What is celebrated is repeated.

Your willingness to embody the vision ... will have a direct impact on your credibility.

Making your vision stick requires boldness. It will require you to develop a healthy intolerance for those things that have the potential to impede your progress.

True Change that

Lasts *"If you don't have the outcomes you*

desire,

---

personal change is needed in order to alter those outcomes.

Great change is needed if you want great outcomes."

Andy Andrews[19]

In **The Chosen Marriage** seminar[20], I discuss the state of marriage and relationships, and of course, how to change them. No one comes to a marriage seminar unless they are seeking some sort of improvement. We would casually call this change. But change is not casual; change is hard, especially for human beings. Change means exchanging one thing for another. So, all change requires something to be given up.

232 The Renewed Mind

Perhaps this is passive giving up, but it's giving up none the less.

Consider, if you are single, you are free to do whatever you want, within the law and acceptable social constraints. You are essentially free. Free to decide, free to travel, free to eat, live, or play where you choose. Free to be a great person, free to be a complete knucklehead. Free. But, once you commit to someone as a couple, whether that is dating, engagement, marriage, or cohabitation, you are no longer single. You are now part of a couple, at least as it pertains to choices. Your freedom has been curtailed. But that was a choice.

Now, as a couple, you choose marriage and to raise a family. Once a child is born, your *coupleness* changes. No longer is it the two of you together doing whatever the two of you want. Now you are parents, a major change in life. And as parents, you must do what the child needs, demands, and creates for you. Your freedom is extremely limited now. But that too, was a choice.

These choices, as are all choices, are things that you decide in the moment about what you would like to see in your life. Most of them are small choices, with limited amount of thought. Others are major choices that require major amounts of thought. But what they both have in common is once the choice is made it's instantaneous. A choice is simply deciding—choosing one thing as opposed to another.

Author Andy Andrews has a way of explaining major life principles in simple stories. One of my favorite examples is a series of stories around a central character called *Jones*. In those stories, among other things, he talks about decisions to change. His focus in his story is on gaining perspective. Usually, it's perspective that we are missing that causes us to make mistakes or to make poor choices. Andrews explains in his story across a trilogy of books that the *decision for change* is instantaneous, but that is not enough to bring about actual change. According to Andrews[21] it goes something like this:

1. The decision to change doesn't take long. The time leading up to the decision may be long. Someone *decides* to change in the space of a heartbeat—in that moment when they conclude that they truly want that change. In that moment of decision, it is established instantaneously. The process to make that decision can take a very long time. But once the process is complete, the decision is immediate. But that decision will not change the outcomes in life. After the decision, there must be action.

2. Once activated by commitment, change becomes dramatic. True Change takes action to ACTIVATE. The practice (of those actions) takes more time, along with your own acceptance of the truth of your change. Perhaps a lot of time if the change is critical to your wellbeing. It takes time for you to practice and rehearse your chosen change consistently. In marriage, change is often essential to the short- and long-term success of the relationship. Change is often demanded, at times selfishly, by one partner or the other. At other times, the need for a change is obvious or needed to resolve ongoing disputes or failures. And then other times, change is required to meet a shared perceived outcome or goal.

If, as a couple, you decide that you want to own your own home, as a couple you must make a lot of *strategic* decisions, often involving many painful sacrifices. The decision to own a home comes quickly. For some, it's even a forgone conclusion that this is what you must achieve. For others, it comes from deep thought about the pros and cons of renting versus owning. Whether the decision took many thoughtful discussions over a long time, or was made quickly, the decision is now made. It has become instantaneously decided. But no house is going to appear just because of your decisions.

Your decision requires an effort to *put into action* the strategies (behaviors) that will most likely produce that outcome you have decided is the one you want. Cutting back on spending and forcing financial discipline to save enough for a down payment, staying steadily employed and stable for two or more years to help prove your ability to repay a loan, and of course, timely payment of bills and low levels of debt to raise your FICO score. All of these are actions, based on your decision, which will likely produce the outcome of home ownership. But without those actions, you are unlikely to be successful.

Making your decision is the first step to real, or lasting change. But it is only one step. It does nothing on its own. A decision to change is not enough. I recall when I was a junior in high school, I was very envious of my sister and her friends. All of them played some sort of instrument, and like a lot of teens at the time, they formed a garage band. I was consumed with envy. So, I took up the guitar, and failed. Then the bass failed. Vocals, forget that. In the end, I failed to achieve any sort of inclusion in this group. It was not the decision to act that was at fault, and it was not even the early actions I took, acquiring instruments and books. It was the *conviction* of my decision to drive long-term action; practice and fortitude to endure the challenge was lacking. You see, a decision to act is not enough to foster change. Actions must also take place. But action alone is not enough.

There are three types of action that must occur if the action stage of change is lead to True Change. Action must be *appropriate, consistent,* and *timely*.

Appropriateness is simply doing the right thing in the moment that it needs doing. My favorite examples for life tend to be based on driving experiences here in Hampton Roads. If you're familiar with our area of Virginia, you will know that people drive as if there is no one else on the road that matters to them. However, we have a basic rule though that we all agree to follow—we do not cross the double yellow line. This keeps everyone alive. If you are *appropriate* in your driving, you will be on your side of the double yellow line while other people are coming from the opposite direction. If you are not appropriate in this action, and cross the line, unfortunate things are likely to happen. Being appropriate is doing the right thing in the right way *at the right time*. The example that I give in parenting class is, if your child needs their diaper changed and is crying from discomfort, but you rush in and stick a bottle in their mouth and call it good, you have failed the child in that moment. Appropriate is necessary. Regarding your recovery, you need to remain appropriate in your actions regardless of the feedback that you get from your wife or others. You need to do the right things whether she is noticing or not. Having integrity means doing the right thing even when no one else is looking, even if you know you won't get caught if you don't.

Consistency is necessary as well. Consistency builds habits. Once habits become automatic, your character will be altered. Character is the outward demonstrated to others of what is otherwise and inward process of thoughts, feelings, and choices. In week one, we used the cognitive behavioral Choice Cycle to illustrate how what people see as our characters is actually an external demonstration of our repeated internal process and how actions lead to habits. Habits are the constant behavioral choices we make. So, doing the right thing is absolutely necessary. But doing it *consistently* will build a new set of habits, and profound changes will be dramatic in your character demonstration which *over time*, others can recognize and appreciate.

Timeliness has two components. First there is the *immediacy*. Doing the right thing, being appropriate, you need to do it in the moment required. It is not the *right thing* if you don't do it at the *right time*. The old English proverb warning about the futility of closing the barn doors after the horses escaped applies here. This proverb warns that trying to do something, *after a problem has occurred*, is futile. You need to be proactive before disaster comes.

Timeliness means to be on time. But it also means something else. It means to *continue over time* with the same appropriate and consistent behavior. Time, they say, heals all wounds. This is true when there has been a betrayal trauma in your relationship. Your spouse needs to see your appropriate and consistent change over *a prolonged period* to accumulate enough evidence for her to reactivate some level of willingness to offer trust and respect once more. And perhaps that's the hardest part for most men to deal with, that long-term without acknowledgement or reward for their change efforts.

If you have betrayed your spouse, acknowledge that it will take a lot of time for the *consistency* of your *actions* to *prove* to your wounded spouse that your *commitment* to change is not only real, but will also *last*, and she is no longer unsafe. With big change, your challenge comes from inside and outside. Your internal process is something we have been working on for the past 16 weeks. But the bigger challenge to change is to provide external evidence to a level that it can be viewed, accepted, and then trusted, by your wife. No matter how much *you believe* in your change, she can't see your heart. She can only see it in your behavior. And if you do not form the proper habits over a long period of time, then she cannot trust that the previously established character that she's come to know so well has truly changed.

The inability of others to acknowledge and affirm your changes in the short run can become the biggest challenge to your sobriety and success. The speed at which your spouse and others are willing to acknowledge and trust your change is not going to come anywhere near *your* perceived success rate. While your internal change happened in an instant, and you sincerely believe the decision if firm and well established, and even self-evident in the new actions you practice which clearly demonstrate proof of that change, acceptance by others *will* take a very long time, especially if you have damaged their trust. For a betrayed spouse, acceptance and trust is delayed over time, equal to the amount to the amount of time you spent proving to her your unreliable character and the level of damage you have done. John Gottman tells couples that there is a *magic ratio* of five to one for restoration. For each hurt you caused, you must do five good things to make a repair (paraphrased).

This is why I've taken you through so many levels of understanding in *The Renewed Mind* process. Your outcome goals must become and stay bigger than your immediate goals. If your goal is big, and well informed, and the change is true, it will endure the test of time. Recall the week one cycle, "if you don't like your outcomes, change your character, habits, actions, feelings, thoughts, beliefs..." You need to focus now, and for the rest of your life, on the outcomes you want. Not the momentary pleasures of life. They will come on their own with good choices. Outcomes accumulate *over time*, with effort and strategic actions.

Congratulations!

You have made it to the end, which means you are more than likely to complete the process of Renewing your Mind against the scourge that is porn. If you went through a group or used the workbook as a companion guide to this program throughout to process the learning points, you should have discovered a great deal about yourself and the enormity of your life in general, and the specifics of why porn has become such a problem. This is the week we celebrate and declare the future as you have now envisioned it.

If you took the instruction seriously, chose healthy and effective accountability partners, and allowed yourself to be coached or counseled along the way, you should have capped off your experience with the Man of Valor mission. This is more than a simple thought exercise. It is specifically designed to help you to recapture what was lost on a much larger scale than just solving cyber-addiction. The Man of Valor is a man who has recognized his own value and purpose through the eyes of God. A value and purpose that the Man of Valor was created for.

When a man has a strong vision of himself, there is truly little the world, or the enemy, can do to defeat him. Vision is the drive that tells you if you are on the right path. Unlike Alice in Wonderland, you know where you are heading, so the crossroads do not cause stress, anxiety, or confusion. Life becomes simple as you choose *being* yourself over *doing* a role. Being comes naturally. But to be what? Be the vision of that Man of Valor, practice it, honor it, and insist on it so that when the crossroads come, you can simply *be* consistent.

About the Author

Over the years, Dr Chuck has emerged as a preeminent provider for men's pornography recovery and women's *betrayal trauma* recovery in the Hampton Roads region of Virginia, and now has a practice that now extends online around the globe.

Dr Chuck Carrington is a Christian counselor educated in multiple methods of counseling, holding degrees in Human Service Counseling, Mental Health Counseling, Counselor Education and Supervision, and Educational Specialist in Online Learning.

Dr Chuck was awarded the Outstanding Student Award for his work in his early years at Regent University, for research conducted at Old Dominion University by Chi Sigma Iota and recognized for his other research efforts from VACES in Virginia.

If You Need Counseling or Help,

Dr Chuck offers Christian Faith-Based Counseling and Coaching in men's recovery from porn and cyber-addiction, Betrayal Trauma recovery for women, and restorative counseling to help heal and recover marriages after betrayal.

For a consultation via telehealth video, contact Dr Chuck to get more information on how to overcome the damage of betrayal and addiction. Use the website below to sign up for recovery and support groups, or to join Dr Chuck's online psychoeducational programs.

If you are looking for marriage enhancement counseling or coaching, Dr Chuck offers online webinars and forums to help Christian couples explore their marriage, and how it conforms to God's plan for marriage, to find forgiveness and healing, or to plan for an extraordinary marriage from the outset for engaged couples.

Believers should ask for the Faith-based community discount for the best possible pricing. Free groups include Healing Hearts for women damaged by betrayal, Overcomer's Group for men struggling with porn addiction and cyber addiction.

CONNECT

www.connectcounselor.com
Connect Christian Family Counseling
757 965-5450

Check out Dr Chuck's *Seven Greatest Hits in Marriage Counseling*, a series of video supported coaching modules presenting his most effective tools to help couples exceed a typical marriage.

The Renewed Mind: Rebuilding Trust in Marriage by Overcoming Porn Addiction for Life *Workbook* ISBN# ISBN 979-8-9892386-2-0 is available on Amazon at https://a.co/d/fTPdxoO or, log into your Amazon account and search for ASIN: B0CKD2BJJB

www.connectcounselor.com
Connect Christian Family Counseling
757 965-5450
DrChuck@connectcounselor.com
https://connectcounselor.com/group-counseling/

End Notes

[1] Tinbergen N. (1989). *The Study of Instinct.* Clarendon Press; Oxford, UK

[2] Blanchard, K. & Johnson, S. *The One minute manager.*

[3] Greene, R. (2010). *The 33 strategies of war* (Vol. 1). Profile Books.

[4] Covey, S. R. (1991). *The seven habits of highly effective people.* Provo, UT: Covey Leadership Center

[5] Greene, R. (2010). *The 33 strategies of war* (Vol. 1). Profile Books.

[6] *Martin, George R. R. (1996). A game of thrones. New York: Bantam Books*

[7] Greene, R. (2010). *The 33 strategies of war* (Vol. 1). Profile Books.

[8] *Senge, Peter M. (1990). The fifth discipline: the art and practice of the learning organization. New York: Doubleday/Currency.*

[9] Covey, S. R. (1991). *The seven habits of highly effective people.* Provo, UT: Covey Leadership Center

[10] ACE Study. Felitti, V. J., Anda, R. F., Nordenberg, D., Williamson, D. F., Spitz, A. M., Edwards, V., Koss, M. P., & Marks, J. S. (1998). Relationship of childhood abuse and household dysfunction to many of the leading causes of death in adults: The Adverse Childhood Experiences (ACE) Study. *American Journal of Preventive Medicine, 14(4),* 245–258. https://doi.org/10.1016/S0749-3797(98)00017-8

[11] *Martin, George R. R. (1996). A game of thrones. New York: Bantam Books*

[12] Piaget, J., & Cook, M. T. (1952*). The origins of intelligence in children.* New York, NY: International University Press.

[13] Young, *Relationship Schemata.* (Adapted from https://schematherapist.com/18-schemas/)

[14] *Geertz, C. (1973).* "Thick Description: Toward an Interpretive Theory of Culture", *The Interpretation of Cultures: Selected Essays.* New York: Basic Books, pp.3–30

[15] Carroll, L. (2018). *Alice in Wonderland.* Wordsworth Editions.

[16] Maxwell, J. C. (2007). *Failing forward: Turning mistakes into steppingstones for success.* HarperCollins Leadership

[17] Pike, M., Nesfield, V., & Lickona, T. (2015). Narnian Virtues. *Journal of Character Education: Vol. 11# 2, 11*(2), 71-86.

[18] Stanley, A. (?????) Vision stick

[19] Andrews, A. (2009, 2013, 2020). The Noticer Trilogy: The Noticer, The Noticer Returns, Just Jones. New York. Thomas Nelson.

[20] Carrington, C. (2023). The Chosen Marriage (seminar). Downloaded from YOUTUBE: https://youtu.be/2T-kp8oNrZc?si=MwgaA0fLaL1Sg5hD

[21] Andrews, A. (2009, 2013, 2020). The Noticer Trilogy: The Noticer, The Noticer Returns, Just Jones. New York. Thomas Nelson.

Graphics and Images

Feelings Wheel. "Feeling Wheel" by hragv is licensed under CC BY-ND 2.0. To view a copy of this license, visit https://creativecommons.org/licenses/by-nd/2.0/?ref=openverse.

Yellow Brick Road. Photo by Creative Commons, artist unknown.

Made in the USA
Columbia, SC
16 September 2024

41806427R00143